Love Jesus Hate Church

How to **SURVIVE** in Church— or **Die** Trying!

Steve McCranie

BACK2ACTS

PRODUCTIONS

LOVE JESUS, HATE CHURCH
How to *Survive* in Church—or *Die* Trying!
Published by Back2Acts Productions
www.Back2Acts.com

Copyright © 2006 by Steve McCranie
ISBN 0-97715580-0-3
LCCN 2005906884

Author's Note: Some of the names have been changed to protect the identities of the persons involved. Other names and similarities to people living or dead are purely *intentional*— if you know what I mean.

Love Jesus, **Hate Church** may be purchased in bulk for educational, business, fund-raising, or sales promotional use. For information, please email: SpecialEvents@Back2Acts.com.

To receive a *free* monthly **Love Jesus**, **Hate Church** newsletter that will endeavor to keep you informed, encouraged and enlightened as we strive to become more like Christ, please request at our website: www.lovejesushatechurch.com.

For additional **Love Jesus**, **Hate Church** resources, including *free* downloads, please visit our website: www.lovejesushatechurch.com

Printed in the United States of America

03   04   05   06   07

Love Jesus, **Hate Church**
is dedicated to my wife, Karen, and to my children:
Christa, Morgan, Lindsay, Justus, Halcy and, of course, Stacey.
Without them, I doubt I would have ever emerged from my
Love Jesus, **Hate Church** nightmare.
I love each of you!

contents

PART TWO: HOLINESS, CHILD-LIKE FAITH AND OTHER STUFF WE REALLY
DON'T WANT TO TALK ABOUT
How to get out of the nasty mess we have created

PART THREE: PLAYING WITH THE PLAYERS THAT DRESS FOR THE GAME
How to make sure we never get into this nasty mess again

PART FOUR: LOVE JESUS, HATE CHURCH— IN PERSPECTIVE
"What have you learned, Dorothy?"

FINETO: ENDNOTES AND OTHER STUFF THAT BELONGS AT THE END
How to continue your Love Jesus, Hate Church journey

the well-oiled machine

Now to Him who is able to do exceeding abundantly beyond
all that we ask or think, according to the power that works
within us, to Him be the glory in the church and in Christ
Jesus to all generations forever and ever. Amen.
Ephesians 3:20-21

I am saddened by the fact that a book entitled, **Love Jesus, Hate Church**, has to be written.

Its mere existence stands as an incriminating indictment, an irrefutable testimony to the lukewarm, Laodicean times in which we live. **Love Jesus, Hate Church** affirms the vast prevailing darkness that dominates this age and the systemic failure— bordering on criminally negligent failure— of the church to be the "salt and light" Jesus designed and commanded us to be.[1] It's an agonizingly painful look at ourselves and, to quote Jesus, the "height from which we have fallen."[2]

Uh, What Do You Mean When You Say, *Church*?

No, I'm not talking about the *true* church, the *"called-out ones"* Scripture so proudly refers to as "men and women the world was not worthy of."[3] I'm talking about the church of our *own* creation, the church created in our *own* image— our *own* Frankenstein. I'm talking about the man-made institution we call church. You know, the social organization whose steepled buildings dot the landscape of our communities. The club, the structure, the

7

established entity we vainly try to infuse artificial life into each week with our hyped-up praise music, our social programs disguised as ministry, and the self-affirming, feel-good speeches we attempt to pass off as Spirit-empowered sermons.

Or, as those of us who "bear on our bodies the **Love Jesus, Hate Church** battle scars" like to call it— the **Well-Oiled Machine**.

Sound familiar? I thought it might.

These **Well-Oiled Machines** are *everywhere*. Sometimes they're stacked right on top of each other, two or three to a city block, soaking up real estate as soon as it hits the market. They're all known by different names. And each of them holds to a different, yet ever-changing concept of right and wrong in regards to issues such as church government, baptism, modes of prayer, or even styles of worship.

But if we want to be brutally honest with ourselves— they're all pretty much the same.

You know the ones I'm talking about.

They have varied names like Christ Covenant, Harvest Cathedral, Calvary Assembly of God, Freedom Baptist Church, Evergreen Presbyterian Church, St. Paul's UMC, Bethany Worship Center and so forth.

Some of these institutions (I hate to call them *churches* for reasons you'll discover in the next chapter or two) are named to declare their perceived preeminence among the others. Top dog, head honcho type of church stuff.

"After all," smug expression, thumbs hooked in suspenders, chest puffed out, air of arrogance, "we're members of First Baptist, or First Wesleyan, or First Assembly or First *Whatever*"— which would imply that to attend any other church would make you less than...uh, first, I guess.

Does it make you feel the same way?

Others, who obviously weren't first (since that name was already taken by some of the churches listed above) are named to denote their location: Thomas Road Baptist Church, West Franklin Pentecostal Church, Central Church of God— or the Church on the Corner of Main and Maple. Hmmm. Let's just hope that none of these congregations ever have to move.

"I'm a member of the Northeast Church of God which was formally known as Central Church of God. But, it was really called My Little Neighborhood Church of God in the very beginning, way back when. But that was a long time ago before I became a member. And that's my story and I'm stickin' to it."

Now that's quite a mouthful.

Then, of course, there are those institutions that want to be known by their non-negotiable doctrinal distinctives or their statements of faith. In this category you have names such as Evangelical Free, Free Will and anything Baptist, Presbyterian, or with the word Covenant *anywhere* in the name.

We even find some that are named to honor some dead and departed big-time tither or founding pastor or to stand as a monument to the resident "family in charge" such as Hinton or Stowe Memorial.

As Sonny and Cher used to sing, "The beat goes on."

What is the Purpose of Love Jesus, Hate Church?

The purpose of **Love Jesus, Hate Church** is not in any way to slam, malign, tear down, or "dis" the church. Nor is this book designed to simply point out the obvious faults, systemic shortcomings, or the inherent hypocrisy that has plagued the institution of the church for the last millennium and a half.

No, the purpose of **Love Jesus, Hate Church** is actually quite the opposite.

The goal of **Love Jesus, Hate Church** is to present the church in the breathtaking splendor the Lord intended— as the spotless, chaste, virgin bride of Christ. It's to show the church, as Paul so clearly pointed out in Ephesians 3, as the eternal vessel of Christ's glory on earth.

Consider the praise of the Apostle Paul:

> Now to Him who is able to do exceeding abundantly beyond all that we ask or think, according to the power that works within us, to Him be the glory (where) *in the church* and in Christ Jesus to all generations forever and ever. Amen.[4]

The problem we face, however, is the *visible* church that which we see, attend, claim membership to and have known all our lives, is a far cry from the *true* church revealed in Scripture. It's literally light years from the living entity Jesus promised the very "gates of hell will not prevail against."[5] What we see masquerading as church today is, at best, a dim reflection of the Lord's intention. In fact, the current *visible* church that seems to dot every other street corner in North America is now so far removed from the example Jesus left us in Scripture, that we might *never* be able to divorce ourselves from our traditions, and experience the pure bride of Christ in all her fullness.

Or, to put it in the perspective of the Lord's promise to us, we, frankly, may *never* be able to experience the *abundant life* He promised.[6] Never! At least not within our current church structures and religious mindsets.

So what are we to do?

Good question. But we've got a great answer!

Is Love Jesus, Hate Church a Book For Me?

Love Jesus, **Hate Church** was written with several groups of people in mind.

First, it was written as a word of encouragement to the true, sold-out, stand-alone believer in Christ— to the genuine, real deal Christian. The *"called-out ones."*

It is written for those of *you* who will follow Him as long as *you* live. For those of *you* who will proclaim, like the Reformers of old, "Sola Scriptura" and continually testify of His grace and mercy regardless of how the rising apathy of the *church*, the **Well-Oiled Machine**, tries to drown out your voices.[7]

It is written to affirm those of *you* who have genuinely experienced, first hand, His unfathomable love, His unmerited forgiveness, and His peace— the "peace that passes all understanding."[8] Yep, this book was written for *you*. Why? For it's *you* who must now stand and proclaim the truth about what now *is* and what *must be*. It's *you* who must weather the storm from within and without. It's you who... well, I don't want to jump too far ahead at this point.

Needless to say, you *know* who you are.

Next, **Love Jesus**, **Hate Church** was written to those of you who are living large in the land of Laodicea, those of you who have purchased waterfront property by the sea of lukewarmness. Those who, as the Scripture states, have a "form of godliness, but deny its power."[9] Those to whom our Lord said He would vomit out of His mouth.[10]

To you, this book will be an indictment of what church *could be*, and what church *should be*— but *what is* because the personal cost seemed too high. The price for intimacy with Christ was too expensive. Too taxing. Not worth the effort.

It's like saying to Jesus, "Lord, I see Your lips moving, but all I hear is blah, blah, blah."

To you, my prayer is that you will see yourself in these pages and fall on your face in repentance, begging our Lord for another chance to live for Him— and to die to yourself for Him.[11]

Oh, by the way, you also *know* very well who *you* are.

And finally, **Love Jesus, Hate Church** was written for any Believer in Christ that desires to find a congregation that affirms, encourages, builds-up, and "stands together as one man contending for the faith."[12] In other words, if you've ever been hurt by church or if you sometimes only go because it's the inane "right thing to do"— boy, do we have some good news for you!

You can be different.

You can model the New Testament prototype of the church to others.

Things don't have to stay the same! The past doesn't have to repeat itself.

For you, be encouraged! **Love Jesus, Hate Church** is written to show you how church life ***can be***, and ***will be***, when we put God first and ***everything*** else second.

Are you curious? Interested? Good.

Then what are you waiting for?

Go ahead, take a deep breath, count to three— and jump right on in.

the joy of believing the lie

Truth, even from the lips of a deceased, foul-mouthed
comic— is still truth.

"Every day people are straying away from the church and
going back to God."
Lenny Bruce (1926-1966)

When I was a kid, church seemed to be a picture of the kind of family
I always wanted. The kind of family I didn't have at home. I remember
Sunday school and youth outings and pot-luck fellowship dinners that were
served by large, overweight women with large, inviting smiles. I remember
Vacation Bible School and the Church Softball League and the addictive
feeling of oneness I experienced when I was with my other co-patriots in
the youth department. It was like I finally belonged to something— like
I had finally found a home. A purpose. *Something* I could believe in and
somebody I could trust.

Oh yeah, I remember *all* the good stuff. All the Christ-like stuff.

The kind of stuff that leads a young boy like me to dream of becoming
a pastor someday— of devoting his life to the Lord.

Ah, such sweet, childlike innocence.

Such blessed ignorance.

The *joy* of *believing* the lie.

Yeah, right.

13

It's like living in a Norman Rockwell painting...uh, until the day your balloon bursts and you lose your church virginity and your whole world comes crashing down around you.

Oh, I remember all the *good* stuff.

But I also remember all the *not-so-good* stuff.

The stuff nightmares are made of.

I'm not sure when my blinders came off and I began to see, for the first time, the church for what it actually is. Try as I may, I simply can't pinpoint the specific situation or the event or maybe even the conversation that began my long descent from idyllic bliss into the cold, dark, painful reality of church. I can't put my finger on the exact day when I lost my spiritual virginity and began to **Love Jesus** and **Hate Church**.

But it happened.

Slowly at first, like a tiny trickle from a leaky faucet. Small. Insignificant. Hardly worth mentioning.

Drip after drip after horrid drip— until it pounded in my brain like the incessant beating of the old man's heart in Poe's, *Tell-Tale Heart.*[1]

And before I could turn around, by default, I had joined the ever-swelling ranks of those who **Love Jesus** and **Hate Church**. I had become one of *them.* I was now joined at the hip, like a Siamese twin, to a group of people I didn't even know existed.

But I know now. Boy, do I know *now!*

Love Jesus and **Hate Church**? Sound impossible? Contradictory?

Well, it's not.

My life stands as irrefutable proof of these two realities— **Love** and **Hate** and **Jesus** and **Church** all in the same sentence.

Confession: I **Love Jesus** with a burning, all-consuming passion. He is the source of my life and the *best* thing that has ever happened to me. In a word, I am literally *obsessed* with Him.[2]

But make no mistake, I **Hate Church** and *everything* it has become today. I **Hate Church** with a raw, loathing vengeance, with unleashed rage, with every fiber in my being. It's like church pushes me right to the edge, right to the point of no return— and then sadistically pushes even harder, mocking, sneering, and demanding I respond.

Sometimes it scares me. My rage. I didn't know I had the capacity to hate that much.

But I do.

And the focus of that hate is what *so-called* Christians have done to the Church in the name of Christ![3]

Come On, You Know It's True

You've heard the rumors, the depressing tales of woe, the never-ending classic late-night horror stories about good people hurting good people in church. Maybe you've got a couple of stories of your own to tell. Maybe you've got your own church scars. Maybe you've got your own reasons for those countless sleepless nights. Maybe you've been the victim of a vicious, well-organized, rape, pillage, and burn campaign that often takes place behind so-called sanctified church walls.

Maybe you've got your own reasons— darn good reasons, to **Love Jesus** and **Hate Church**.

Maybe. Just maybe.

On the other hand, maybe *you're* the reason someone else has a story to tell. Maybe *you're* the one who held the knife that cut and scarred the tender spirit of another with your gossip, pride, or unmasked hypocrisy. Maybe you're the one, drunk behind the wheel of self-righteousness, that plowed his car headlong into the crowd of bystanders one Sunday morning, wounding and maiming the innocent with your misplaced anger.

"I don't care what the pastor says, we've been here longer than he has. He'd better start listening to *us* if he knows what's good for him."

"Did you see the dress Martha was wearing? Who's she trying to impress?"

"Frank always gets to sing lead in the Easter Cantata. What makes him think he's *that* good?"

"Where did all these *new* people come from? Who invited them to *our* church anyway?"

Maybe you've got blood on your own hands.
Maybe you're the Pilate in your own church.
Maybe you're one of the ones that shouted, "Give us Barabbas!"
Maybe.
Just maybe.

a conversation with josh

"I'm completely in favor of the separation of Church and
State. My idea is that these two institutions screw us up
enough on their own, so that both of them together
is certain death."
George Carlin (1937-)

Recently, I had a conversation with a young, impressionable, 23 year
old college student named Josh who attends a Baptist church located close to
the buckle on the Bible belt. Over the past few months he had been sharing
with me some of his concerns with his home church or, more accurately,
with the church leadership. According to Josh, his church seemed like a *nice*
church. I mean, everything seemed to be going well (whatever that means)
until about two months ago.

The Youth Pastor they had was doing a great job with the teenagers.
He was liked by virtually all of the parents, and the church as a whole was
genuinely pleased with the spiritual progress and numerical growth they
were experiencing in the Youth Department. And then, out of nowhere, the
unthinkable happened. Bang!— his wife left him.

No warning.

No "bogie at two o'clock."

No Doppler radar weather map.

Nothing.

Just, here this morning. Gone tonight.

So the Youth Pastor, understandably devastated by the hand dealt him, did what he believed to be the Biblical and, ironically, the spiritually mature thing to do. He came directly to his pastor and the deacons of the church and explained the turmoil he was going through.

"You know, I'm having some serious marital problems," he began with a deep sorrow in his voice. "My wife has left me and, right now, I'm really in no state to continue to lead the youth. I desperately need you, and the church, to pray for me and my wife and my family. I also need to step down from my position of leadership in the church for a while in order to work out my problems at home. Can the church give me some time, a sabbatical, to get my home life in order?"

Well, do you know what the church did? Guess. Did they wrap their arms around this broken man in Christian compassion, empathy, and love? Did they earnestly assure him of their continued help and understanding during his time of crisis? Did they promise to lift him and his wife up in prayer, seeking and begging God for a restoration in their marriage and his ministry? Hey, did they even *pray* with him after he confessed the deep fears of his heart to his own pastor and deacons?

Of course not.

They fired him! Bam! "Hit the road, Jack! You're outta here, Bub! Don't let the door hit you in the butt on your way out!" Why? "Well, we can't have any staff members associated with this church, with *our* church, struggling with personal issues or marital problems. Heck, no. People may get the idea we all have some sort of problems and are less than perfect— and, we can't have that. Why, it's unthinkable. After all, we have a reputation in the community to think of."

As expected, this whole series of sad, tragic events left the teenagers and many of their parents shocked, dismayed and bewildered as to why the church leadership, and especially their pastor, would respond to a desperate cry for help this way. Needless to say, one by one, Sunday by Sunday, like a slow leak in a rubber raft, the youth group just drifted away. But as the politically correct, point the finger, take no blame, best foot forward, church spin machine kept reminding themselves with their gossip-disguised press releases…

For Immediate Release: The rapid demise of the youth group had to be the fault of the recently separated, currently unemployed, emotionally disenfranchised, former Youth Pastor. It is *not* the fault of the church or its leadership. We categorically deny any responsibility. Our hands are clean. We did nothing wrong.

Yeah, right.

This poor youth pastor came and Biblically shared his struggles and heartaches with his church family, with those who had earlier stood alongside him in committed ministry. He passionately begged for their prayers, help, understanding, and compassion. He cried out for someone, *anyone*, to simply "bear his burden" like he, as a minister, had borne the burdens of others in the past. And just like that, they fired him!

Sad, isn't it? But quite typical of most of the churches I've personally been associated with.

Is it any wonder why this young man, striving to keep his marriage together and his faith intact, **Loves Jesus** and **Hates Church**?

Makes you think, doesn't it?

the good, the bad, and the very ugly

"The more I study religions the more I am convinced that
man never worshiped anything but himself."
Sir Richard Francis Burton (1821-1890)

Dietrich Bonhoeffer, the German martyr, theologian, and patriot
who gave his life at the hands of Henrich Himmler's Gestapo at the
Flossenburg concentration camp on April 9, 1945, was once confronted
with his personal evaluation of the lasting impact of his own book, *The Cost
of Discipleship*. He was asked, from the position as both a Believer and a
proud member of the German aristocracy, how he perceived the relevance of
the church and its place in society. Does the church have a place in modern,
enlightened society? Is it relevant? Or has it outlived its usefulness?

These plaguing questions, presented to Dietrich shortly before his
death, give rise to the very question each of us must ask ourselves from
the standpoint as both Believers in Christ, those "chosen in Him from the
foundation of the world",[1] and as those presently living in the decadence and
unparalleled apathy of the New Millennium.

Living, if you will, in the spiritual land of Laodicea.[2]

The question is quite simple.

But your answer will change the very course of your life and the way
you view everything.

Do you believe the church can literally change society?
Or, to put it another way…
Do you truly believe the church can make a difference?

Now, your answer is going to be either "Yes" or "No".
Let's take a look at both.

For the "Yes" Category:

If your answer is an emphatic, "*Yes*, (which I hope all of us would affirm) I *do* believe the church can make a difference in our society and world"— then the natural follow-up question would be, "Well, why is it not happening?" Why is our society and our culture, our very lives and the lives of our families, the collective morals and conscience of the neighborhoods we live in— why are they slipping further and further away from the truth? If it's possible and actually expected for the church to be the definitive change agent in the lives of people *and* if Jesus truly came to "give life, and give it abundantly" as He said— then why, in fact, is it not taking place?[3]

What's the problem?

Where's the hold-up?

What or who is standing in the way?

Where's the evidence of the power Jesus delegated to those who are called by His name? Why do we seem impotent against the swarming tide of darkness when Scripture clearly states that "greater is He who is in us than he who is in the world"?[4] To quote an old, classic Wendy's commercial— "Where's the beef?" I mean, if we truly believe the church can change the lives of our family, friends, and neighbors, but find it's not happening— well, let me ask you Church, "Where's the beef?"

For the "No" Category:

Or, if your honest answer to the probing question is, "*No*, I don't believe the church can make any permanent or visible difference in society"— then our logical follow-up question to you would be, "So, why do you go to church? Why are you reading this book? What's the point of coming together every Sunday and falsely proclaiming to live out what you really don't believe? Who are you trying to fool? Who are you trying to impress? Why would you want to hang around a bunch of losers— a bunch of people as spiritually unfruitful and powerless as you are? Let's face it, if

24

you don't believe God can use the church, or use us *as* His church, to change the lives of the people Jesus died for, then why in the world are you wasting your time and God's resources with the whole hypocrisy of church?"

I mean, what's the point?

Hey, Who's Fault is it Anyway?

Ah, the $1,000,000 question in our religious "Who Wants to be a Millionaire" church blame game. But please understand, the church has long since exhausted all its lifelines!

So, now to the *one*, final follow-up question. The *one* question that delves deepest into the tender quick of our true commitment to Christ and the *one* question that reveals the most to us, about us, and exposes who we are and what we really value. It's the *one* vital question each of us must ask ourselves in this **Love Jesus**, **Hate Church** religious limbo we often find ourselves.

Are you ready? Then let's cut to the chase.

Experience: If we *do* believe God can change the world through the church and that nothing is impossible with Him,[5] but our lifelong experience clearly shows us that this is not what's happening…

Question: Then why do we foolishly persist in believing in church? Why do we keep attending every Sunday? Why do we continue to subject ourselves to the disappointment of an institution that makes big promises but never delivers?

Application: I mean, isn't that like putting a pocket full of quarters into a Wal-Mart drink machine that only takes our money and never delivers what it promises? Come on, who in their right mind would continue to do that?

First time, shame on you. Second time, shame on me.

Think for a moment, what's the problem with the mission of the church? Why can't the church seem to fulfill her calling? Why does the church seem powerless to realize her destiny? Where does the fault lie?

Is It God?

Is the problem with Him, with God?

Is He somewhat deficient, selfish, or unfair in the giving of His gifts? Did the early church somehow have something the Lord has chosen to keep from us? Is He playing favorites? Were they more blessed than we are today? Did the abundant life only apply to the larger-than-life figures within the pages of Scripture or do they also apply to those of us who "believed in Him through their word."[6] Did they have a special power or anointing, a direct DSL line to the Lord, while we suffer with an outdated and overloaded 28.8 dial-up prayer modem?

Is the problem really with the Lord?

Is It Us?

Or, is the problem with us?

Is the lack of power within the church related to the way we view Scripture or with our personal lack of faith, devotion and evangelism? Maybe our failure as the church is directly related to the times or dispensation in which we live or maybe it's just the logical result of our years of generational apathy. Is the problem found in our pride, selfishness, greed, or our own lack of common caring? Have we as Christians, as the church, let the fruit of the seed of Christ become choked out and unfruitful by the "worries of this world and the deceitfulness of wealth"?[7] Have we failed to diligently heed what Jesus warned us about in the Sermon on the Mount? What's wrong with us? How can we change? Do we really want to change?

Wow. It's not supposed to be this way!

Same Church, Different Sunday

Remember Josh from the last chapter? He's the young guy that goes to the church that fired their youth director for having some problems with his home life.

Remember? Ah, I thought so.

Josh was telling me about another sobering **Love Jesus**, **Hate Church** situation that took place one Sunday morning in June when his church had a graduation recognition service in lieu of a time of worship.

Sidebar: Now, I'm not exactly sure why a church would devote time specifically reserved for the worship and adoration of the Lord to the recognition of graduating high school seniors. But stranger things have happened and there's a lot about church I don't understand. To me, it seems akin to scheduling a Tupperware party during your little girl's birthday bash. Imagine the disappointment on your daughter's face when she realized her special day wasn't really special at all. We just used it as an excuse to do something we wanted to do, something that was beneficial to us, regardless of how it made her feel.

Anyway, that's a topic for another day and another chapter.

Josh began our conversation with a look of concern and dismay on his face.

"Man, my preacher didn't even get a chance to preach last Sunday!"

"Why not?"

"Well, they had the graduation recognition on Sunday. There were four people who graduated and the lady in charge got up and talked about how great and wonderful the kids were that were graduating. She talked for almost an hour! By the time our pastor got up to preach, there was like only 5 minutes left in the service and he simply told everyone he didn't have time to preach. So he just closed the service. He said that God had given him a message and he couldn't preach it in five minutes. He just closed his Bible, prayed and we went home. You know, I kinda felt sorry for him."

Really? Plot thickens. "This, my dear Watson, needs further investigation."

So I asked Josh a couple of questions.

"Why didn't the pastor cut the graduation part of the service short? Why didn't he just smile and say, 'Hey, thanks a lot. We appreciate what you've said about these fine young men and women— let's give our graduates a round of applause,' and then move on? Why did he sit back and do nothing?"

"Simple," Josh said, "because if my pastor did *that* to the lady up front passing out all the stuff and doing all the talking, well, you see, she's part of one of the *key* families in the church. She's hooked in real tight. If our pastor did *that*, man, there'd be *hell* to pay. If you know what I mean "

Yes, Josh. Unfortunately, I know *exactly* what you mean.

Is it a Church Serve-*Us* or a Church Service?

A couple of days later I ran into Josh at the corner Food Lion. He was still smarting over some of the **Love Jesus, Hate Church** skirmishes that had gone down in his church over the past several months. They really bothered him. And, no matter how hard he tried, he couldn't seem to make much sense out of good people hurting good people in the so-called name of the Lord. But Josh wasn't alone in what he was feeling. I can't seem to make much sense out of it either. Can you?

"Hey, Josh," I asked. "Do you *worship* in your church?"

"I think so," he said, looking puzzled. "Well, I guess I really don't know what you mean by *worship*."

"Sure you do, Josh. On Sunday mornings when your church comes together, do you *worship* the Lord? You know, do you lose yourself in sheer adoration of Jesus? When you come to church is there a spirit of the awe of God, a spirit of God's power— a spirit of oneness and community with Christ that moves in your service? Do you feel you are, as Jesus said, 'the kind of worshipers the Father seeks as His worshipers'?[8]

"Come on, Josh, think about it. When your church comes together to worship do they passionately express their love and gratitude to Jesus for all He has done for them? I mean, do they get excited or reverent when they think about Jesus? In other words, do you truly *worship* in your church?"

By this time, Josh was looking a bit confused. No wonder. These were tough questions being tossed his way. How would you have answered them?

"Or," as I tried to elaborate, "when you come together on Sundays, do you simply sit and sing a couple of songs that, quite honestly, some people in your church like and others don't? Do you pretty much do the same thing and go through the same motions, over and over again, every time you come together? Is Sunday morning the time your church has purposely set aside and dedicated *solely* for the worship and adoration of the Lord? Nothing more. Just worship. Just Him.

"If so, then what's that time like? What's the time of worship like in your church? Is it powerful and exciting? Can you feel the presence of the Lord in your midst like they did in the wilderness when God literally walked through their camp? Are you spiritually or emotionally moved when your church worships? Are you moved at all? About anything? Is your time of worship at least as exciting as a Newsboys concert?

"Or, if you were brutally honest with yourself— is church sometimes boring? Out of touch? Does it often feel like a big waste of time?"

The blank, open-mouth stare on Josh's face showed me he wasn't exactly getting the meaning of what I was trying to ask him. Actually, he looked like I'd just slapped him.

So to illustrate the mundane routine that we often confuse and mislabel as worship every Sunday, I asked Josh a few, final questions.

"Josh, about your Sunday service…"
"Yeah. What about it?"
"Does your church take up an offering on Sunday?"
"Sure. Doesn't every church?" Sarcasm.
"Is it near the middle of the service or at the end?"

"Middle. Right before the sermon."

"Do the ushers walk down the aisle to the front of the church to pick up the offering plates?"

Josh nodded, yes.

"And do they play some sort of organ music while the offering is being received by the ushers?"

"Yeah…" drawled Josh with a hint of 'have you been to my church before?' in his voice.

"After they take up the offering, do the ushers walk back down to the front of the church in solemn little groups, military style, to present it to the church? Or do they just stash the cash somewhere in the back and count it later?"

"No, they walk down together and put the plates back on the offering table."

"Then it's time for the choir performance or some sort of *special* music, right?"

"Uh, right."

Smiling, I said, "Suppose one Sunday your pastor stood up and said, 'God has really impressed upon me today that He wants us to give to Him our total devotion this morning. He wants us to focus on Him and Him alone. He wants us to give Him our very best!' (Ah, I can see the varied graying and balding heads begin to nod up and down in agreement all over the congregation. After all, who wouldn't agree with giving God our very best— especially in *our* church)?

But, as not to get totally sidetracked, we'd better move on.

'To give our Lord our very best in worship,' the pastor continued, 'we're just going to sing to Him for 30 minutes this morning. If you want to join with us, great! Then I want to preach the message to you I believe God has given me and then we're going to close with a time of prayer. That's all. Nothing else. No distractions. We're not going to have any announcements that may take our focus off Him. No interruptions. Today, we're going to try to just totally focus on God. If you have an offering to give, the ushers will be at the back of the church after the service so you can drop it in the plate on your way out.'

"What would happen, Josh," I asked, "if your pastor did something like what I just described to you one Sunday morning?"

Without hesitation, "They'd run him off. He'd be gone."

"Why?"

"Because, you just can't come up and surprise everybody and change a service like that. The offering, I mean, that's like way too important to be messin' with. If my pastor tried something like that, man… as much as I love him… he'd be history!'"

Is this for Preaching? Or, for Living?

Some of you may laugh at this example because you don't have ushers in your church or maybe you take up the offering at the end of the service and not in the middle. Maybe your church doesn't even have an organ, or somebody who can carry a tune. Maybe you laugh because you assume that when you come together to worship each Sunday you're not at all like Josh's church. You're different. You're spiritual. You're better.

Maybe so.

Then again, maybe not.

But my question to each of you is the same as it was to Josh.

When your church comes together to worship— do *you* worship?

Do you truly lose yourself in the sheer adoration of the Lord?

Do you offer to Him the unsoiled praises of your lips, the clean hands of faithful service, and a heart filled with a love for others?

Or, do you sing some songs that occasionally you like and enjoy and, more often than not, you don't?

After your time of worship each Sunday, have *you* connected with God?

Have *you* been inspired to Godly living?

Have *you* been rebuked or corrected by His Word?

Have *you* been encouraged by the depth and breath of His Holy Spirit?

Have *you* been exhorted as a Believer to strive for the deeper things of the Spirit?

Have *you* really focused on God and God alone?

Have *you* experienced God's presence in your worship service? If so, great! If not, why? Why do you still pack the kids in the minivan and cart them off to church? Why waste your time? Why on earth are you doing this? What's the point?

Why do you waste your time in church half-heartedly hoping that God will show up when you could just as easily bring Him with you every time you come?

Do you believe your church can change society? And, if so, why is it not happening?

The Good, the Bad and the Very Ugly

There's a simple truth in Scripture that is often overlooked— even *purposely* overlooked in all the **How to Build the Church** self-help verbiage that seems to be the rage today in American church circles. Everyone who has started, or pastored, or once attended, or even driven by a so-called "mega" church can't wait to print their own version of a *12 Step Church Growth Program* fast enough to satisfy all the hungry readers who long for shortcuts to spiritual blessings.

"Hey, if it worked for Saddleback in California, it should work for us right here in Dothan, Alabama. Right?"

Well, not exactly.

Church growth is not a matter of duplicating what one pastor did in one setting and expecting, even demanding, the same results in another. It's not a simple matter of diligently applying a set of *Church Growth Principles*, *Group Dynamic Studies*, or *Church Duplication Methods* learned in seminary or by attending a seminar and just kicking back and expecting the Lord to bless as He may have done in the past.

No, it's just not that simple.

If it was, then we would all want to emulate the first church— the Acts 2 church— the example of the church the Lord left for us in Scripture to serve as our role model and prototype. And that's a hard act to follow! Face it, no one in America wants to "sell their possessions and give to any in need" like they did even though we claim we want the blessing they received from that kind of sacrifice.[9] I haven't seen the line forming in church for *that* kind of total commitment. Have you?

Fact is, there's a basic truth Jesus spoke about that is conspicuously missing, AWOL, in our midst. One simple truth that will literally change everything we know and have ever experienced about being a member of His Body— a member of His Church.

It's the *one* truth that can totally rearrange the landscape and refocus the vision of what we commonly call "church" today?

And, if you're totally honest with yourself, you'd have to admit our Sunday landscape needs some changing— especially when that changing comes from the mouth of our Lord Himself.

Let's begin our **Love Jesus, Hate Church** journey by examining that truth.

church sucks!—and other prophetic bumper stickers

"I still say a church steeple with a lightening rod on top
shows a lack of confidence."
Doug McLeod

"Honk if You Love Jesus"
"Real Men Love Jesus"
"In Case of Rapture, this Vehicle Will be Unmanned"
"Jesus. Don't Leave Earth Without Him"
"Follow Me to Church"
"If it's Not the King James, it's Not the Bible!"

Recognize these? Did you know that some of these popular, religious bumper stickers are actually prophetic in nature?

Church Sucks? You've Got to be Kidding!

Before we dive in any deeper let me take a paragraph or two to clear up a few key points and answer a few nagging questions you might have.

First, I understand some of you are probably already a bit put off by the title of this chapter— maybe even a little offended. I'm also keenly aware of the fact that using the word "suck" in the same sentence with the word "church" is troubling to many of you.

It feels sacrilegious. Unholy. Somehow just plain wrong.

Come to think of it, I'll bet some of you are already beginning to experience some emotions that may have lain dormant for a long time. Unsettling emotions. Strong emotions.

Emotions that are hard to deal with and difficult to compartmentalize.

And just think, this is only chapter three! We've got a long way to go.

So let me begin by saying, "Good! What you're feeling is *not* wrong. It's exactly the reaction we were banking on."

"Why?" you ask.

Because the state of the church in our society today is troubling, to say the least. Actually, to be brutally honest early in our **Love Jesus, Hate Church** journey, I also find it nauseating. Stomach churning.

Or, to quote the Lord, "lukewarm" and worthy of being vomited out of His mouth.[1]

Let me ease your mind by stating at the very beginning, before we go any further, that I **do not** believe the church sucks. Nothing, in fact, could be further from the truth. As we stated in the preface, the purpose of **Love Jesus, Hate Church** is not in any way to slam, malign, tear down, or "dis" the church. Nor is this book designed to simply point out the obvious faults, systemic shortcomings, or the inherent hypocrisy that has plagued the institution of the church for the last millennium and a half.

No, the purpose of **Love Jesus, Hate Church** is actually quite the opposite.

The goal of **Love Jesus, Hate Church** is to present the church in the breathtaking splendor the Lord intended— as the spotless, chaste, virgin bride of Christ. It's to show the church, as Paul so clearly pointed out in Ephesians 3, as the eternal vessel of Christ's glory on earth.

Once again, consider the praise of the Apostle Paul:

> Now to Him who is able to do exceeding abundantly
> beyond all that we ask or think, according to the power
> that works within us, to Him be the glory (where) *in*
> *the church* and in Christ Jesus to all generations
> forever and ever. Amen.[2]

The problem we face, however, is the *visible* church— that which we see, attend, claim membership to and have known all our lives, is a far cry from the *true* church revealed in Scripture. It's literally light years from the living entity Jesus promised the very "gates of hell will not prevail against."[3] What we see masquerading as church today is, at best, a dim reflection of the Lord's intention. In fact, the current *visible* church that seems to dot every other street corner in North America is now so far removed from the example Jesus left us in Scripture, that we might *never* be able to divorce ourselves from our traditions and experience the pure bride of Christ in all her fullness.

Or, to put it in the perspective of the Lord's promise to us— we, frankly, may *never* be able to experience the *abundant life* He promised.[4] Never! At least not within our current church structures and religious mindsets.

So what are we to do?

Good question. But we've got a great answer!

The best way for us to understand what Jesus promised about His church is to take a look at it from the vantage point of Scripture and then compare it to what we see marketed as church today. Only then will we be able to see the "heights from which we have fallen."[5] And when we do, we'll conclude that our watered-down, lukewarm, anemic, apathetic excuse for a Spirit-filled living entity... uh... sucks.

"Ah, Grasshopper, now you know where the chapter title comes from."

Ok, let's start our journey together by examining how the true, authentic church of the Bible actually began and how it was designed to function.

The Genesis of the Church

The first mention of this mystery called the *church* came from the very lips of the Lord. Let's take a moment and set the scene so we can take His statement in its full, intended context.

> Jesus said, "I also say to you that you are Peter, and upon this rock *I will build My church*; and the gates of Hades will not overpower it."[6]

It was High Noon in the spiritual OK Corral.

Jesus had just called His twelve disciples to take a stand on exactly who they believed He was. His question to them was pointed, direct, and piercing. Looking around, Jesus asked those who were now called His followers, those who had already left their vocations and families, to verbally commit to what they may have been debating about, possibly even struggling with, in their hearts. It was time for them to get off the fence. Time for them to take a stand.

It was time for them to choose.

The disciples knew what they felt— and what they felt *seemed* right to them. After all, as far back as anyone could remember, no one had ever expounded on the Scriptures the way Jesus had. No one seemed to have the same intimacy with the Word as Jesus did. It was almost like Jesus and God were close, personal friends. Like they were somehow on speaking terms, on a first-name basis. No other "holy man" or rabbi had ever possessed anything close to His power or His authority.

The Spirit of God's Presence upon Jesus was unprecedented. Kinda scary.

The Pharisees and the ruling religious aristocracy paled when compared to this carpenter from Nazareth. Yeah, they all *knew* what they felt about Him. And they *believed* what they felt they knew— at least they thought they did. They just longed for the answer to the *one* question that was foremost on their minds. The question they were afraid to ask. Hesitant to verbalize. That silent, nagging, plaguing, cancer of doubt that held them back from plunging headlong into total commitment to Him. The mental "hedged bet" that called for cautious reserve and shunned reckless abandon.

"Whoa! Hold on, now. Let's not get too excited about all this. Let's just wait and see what happens before we decide to jump in and go public."

The question, simply put, was this: **Who is this Jesus**?

Was He a great teacher? Maybe a miracle worker— like a holy man of old? Was He the One who would lead their country from oppression to freedom? Would He lead a revolution? Would He redeem Israel from the hostile heel of Rome? Was He the One who would finally restore the kingdom to Israel?[7]

Or was there more?

Could He possibly be the One spoken about in the writings of the Law and Prophets?

Was He the anointed One?

Could He truly be the Messiah?

Just who is this Jesus?

Who Do You Say That I Am?

When Jesus and His entourage came into the district of Caesarea Philippi, He began to ask each of them, "Who do people say that the Son of Man is?"[8] Notice how He kept it aloof and non-personal. Just a simple question among friends. "Hey, who is everyone else, not necessarily you, saying that the Son of Man is? Tell me, what have you heard? What's the word on the street?"

The disciples had no problem telling Jesus what they picked up about Him in the marketplace or read about on the internet. Repeating chat room gossip would in no way imply commitment to a position on His identity. No sir. They could answer His question and still hold their own cards close to their chests. You know, play it safe without appearing evasive. "Oh," they replied, "some say you are John the Baptist, others say you are Elijah. Others say you are Jeremiah or another of the prophets."[9]

But Jesus would have no part in their cat-and-mouse game.

With His penetrating, cut-to-the-chase stare, Jesus brought the question from the realm of the academic to the personal. It was not what others believed about Him that mattered any longer. It was now about each of them. It was point blank, first-person, personal.

"But who do *you* say that I am?"[10]

Scripture doesn't record it, but I can imagine a pause, maybe a lengthy pause, between the question of Jesus and the answer given by Peter.

"Who do *you* say that I am?"

Each disciple, one by one, was now forced to look deep into themselves as they tried to come to grips with what they really believed about Jesus. Uncomfortably, they began to eye one another with cutting, quick, side glances— each wondering what the others were thinking. Wondering what the others believed. Wondering who'd be the first to speak. Who'd be the first to blink.

Peter began to stir. He cleared his throat and exhaled deeply.

All eyes were now focused on him, fixed in anticipation. Waiting.

Peter, his head slowly rising.

Peter, looking straight into the eyes of Jesus.

Peter, his gruff voice broken with emotion.

Peter, answering boldly with an emerging confidence.

Peter, from the innermost depths of his heart, said, "You are the Christ, the Messiah, the Son of the Living God."[11]

There. Now it was out. It was finally said. "I said it and I believe it," Peter probably thought. "He is the Son of God."

Can you see it? Can you see what was happening? Faith was in operation here!

Jesus was overwhelmed. He was so impressed with Peter's affirmation of faith in His identity, so pleased with his dogmatic assertion that Jesus was exactly who He had been telling them He was, that He told Peter this truth did not originate from the core of his fisherman's brain or from his prior religious upbringing, whatever that may have been. No, this profound truth, this *single* truth the church was to be founded on— the supreme Lordship of Jesus— was revealed to Peter from the Father above.

Peter had actually heard from God Himself! Wow! Whodathunk?

It was then Jesus spoke the words quoted at the beginning of this chapter. "I will build *My church*, and the gates of Hades shall not overpower it."[12]

Oops! I Said It Again

"Uh, You will build Your what?"

"Church. He said He would build His *church*. I'm sure I heard Him say *church*."

"That's right. I heard it too. He definitely said *church*."

"Church?" the disciples probably thought as they looked at each other with blank expressions on their faces. "Anybody know what a *church* is?"

Seems like people are asking the same question today.

Maybe this would be a good time to take a quick look at the answer.

What is a Church?

The word "*church*" literally means the "*called-out ones*" and specifically refers to a group of people or a defined set of individuals. It does **not** refer to a building or a ministry or a denomination or any of the other stuff we tend to attach to the name today.

Never has.

Never will.

The focus of the "*church*", as Biblically defined, is unashamedly directed towards people and not towards the organization or the man-made structures we associate with the term today. You know, the **Well-Oiled Machine**. Jesus did not give His life for the Southern Baptist Convention or for the Assemblies of God or for any other man-made institution, ministry, organization, or building. He died to pay the penalty for the sins of *people*, individuals just like you and me, regardless of where they happen to attend a Sunday morning service. He shed His blood and invested His life in *people*. And because of His blood investment, when these individuals come together to worship— those redeemed by the blood of the Lord, those who have been given the gift of the Holy Spirit, those snatched from darkness and death to life and light by the bountiful mercy of God— their time together should be *so* uplifting, *so* powerful, *so* awesome with His presence that others will be naturally drawn to them by the sheer joy they see in them.

I mean, isn't that exactly what it was like in the early church?

> They were continually devoting themselves to the apostles' teaching and to fellowship, to the breaking of bread and to prayer. Everyone kept feeling a sense of awe; and many wonders and signs were taking place through the apostles. And all those who had believed were together and had all things in common; and they began selling their property and possessions and were sharing them with all, as anyone might have need. Day by day continuing with one mind in the temple, and breaking bread from house to house, they were taking their meals together with gladness and sincerity of heart, praising God and having favor with all the people. And the Lord was adding to their number day by day those who were being saved.[13]

Jesus had now introduced to the disciples, to the world in fact, this living mystery He called His *church*. But several questions still remained in the minds of those who heard His words.

"When would the church begin? And how?"

"What does a church look like? What does it feel like?"

"What is the function of this church that You said You would build?"

"When are You going to build Your church? And how?"

And finally, "Why do You say that *You* will build *Your* church? What part, if any, do *we* play in the church building plan of Yours?"

More great questions. Let's begin looking at the first and the last in the next chapter. We'll cover the rest in the chapters that follow.

"i can't stop my mouth!"

"With or without religion, you would have good people
doing good things and evil people doing evil things. But for
good people to do evil things, that takes religion."
Steven Weinberg, Nobel Prize Recipient

ACTS - the Infant Church

The book of Acts reveals to us *how* the church was born and *how* it functioned in its infancy. It's **not** designed to be merely an historical record of the struggles and triumphs of a generation of Believers, long since past, whose only value is realized in the realm of academic pursuits. No, the book of Acts serves as an instructive account, a benchmark, an example of how the church functioned in its origin— and how it *should* function now.

Acts is the *one* book in the Bible that God specifically gave to us to demonstrate, not how things were and can never be again— like some frustrating, unobtainable vision or lofty, out-of-reach goal— but as the prototype, the guide, the template, the owner's manual of how a healthy church should function. It's almost like He is telling future generations of Believers, and us today…

"This is how I originally established **My Church**. This is the norm and the standard I have established. When I look at **My Church**, this is what I want to see. And this is how it **CAN** be if you stay focused on Me like those guys were back in the beginning."

Sidebar: Now I know we can spend countless hours debating until dark the concept of cessation by asking the question, "Is the book of Acts simply an account of the early church, or does it apply to us today?" Then, based on our theology, forged primarily by our experience— which usually means the "lack" of power in our lives— we take one side or the other in the continuing saga over the controversy regarding Spiritual gifts, miracles, healings, or whatever.

The discussion tends to go something like this:

"Are the gifts of the Spirit for today or only for those guys back then?"

"Well, if I say they're for today, then you'll want to know why they aren't functioning in my life. You know, why I don't minister in the same power they did back then. Why people aren't being saved daily. Why I don't seem as committed to Christ and to others as the early church was. Geez, I can't have that. It'll make me feel bad. Like I don't measure up or something. So, the gifts of the Spirit must *not* be for today. Definitely not! Otherwise...well...er...I don't want to think about the *otherwise*."

But the one often overlooked point that needs to be stressed is this: Why would Jesus want us to intimately know, by recording it in painstaking detail, how the early church continually ministered with "power from on high" if He never really intended for us to follow in their footsteps?[1] That makes absolutely no sense to me. None. It's like Jesus changed the rules in the first quarter of the game. And that's just not like the Lord.

Why would Jesus prevent the church of today— those of us who claim to be living an abundant, over-the-top, extraordinary spiritual life— from experiencing the power, intensity, and ministry like they did in the pages of the Acts? Why would He allow us to read about others living a life that He, for some reason, is preventing us from living? Why would Jesus purposefully withhold the fullness of the Spirit from us today or only dole it out in small, miserly measures like Ebenezer Scrooge did to Bob Cratchet?

I don't know about you, but that doesn't sound like much of an abundant life to me.

Does it to you?

Anyway, let's get back to Acts.

If you remember, the second chapter of Acts begins by telling us "when the day of Pentecost had come, they were all together in one place."[2] All of a sudden there was the sound of a mighty, rushing wind and tongues of fire came upon each of the disciples. Seeing and hearing the commotion, a great crowd gathered thinking the 120 must be drunk.

Drunk! Yeah, they must have been so giddy, so uninhibited with the love and power of God given to them they appeared to be full of "sweet wine."[3]

Peter, the very one who had previously denied even knowing Jesus, stood up in the midst of this confused and bewildered mass and preached a sermon that is truly a marvel of Old Testament history and New Testament theology. Peter, this gruff, fickle, impulsive, uneducated fisherman from rural Galilee, obediently allowed the Holy Spirit to speak through him, just as Jesus had promised, and an unparalleled, momentous event took place that literally changed the world. Let's face it, Peter's sermon is only several hundred words long: 693 to be exact. If Peter preached this sermon today, even with as much emotion and inflection as he could muster and continually paused for theatrical effect in his best Orson Wells, James Earl Jones, or Sean Connery voice— it still would take less than five minutes to preach. Start to finish. Period.

Peter preached this small, compact sermon with power, strength, and authority that can *only* come from being in the presence of God. Remember, it was with this same Peter that the ruling, religious intelligentsia of the day (that is, smart-bottoms) had some serious problems.

Scripture states, "As *they* (the smart-bottoms) observed the confidence of Peter and John and understood that they were uneducated and untrained men, they were amazed, and began to recognize them as having been with Jesus."[4]

Gosh, wonder if there could have been a connection?

When Peter concluded his five-minute sermon with the statement, "Therefore, let all the house of Israel know for certain that God has made Him both Lord and Christ— this Jesus whom *you* crucified,"[5] the Holy Spirit manifested Himself in convicting power. Pagans, Jews, proselytes, slaves, and just anyone else who happened to be there that day, heard the undiluted Truth in their own language and were "cut to the quick" as they desperately cried out like a chorus of drowning men to Peter and the other Apostles, saying, "Brethren, what shall we do?"[6]

The response was simple, direct, and unchanging. Peter's answer was just as true for them as it is for us today. "Repent, and let each of you be baptized in the name of Jesus Christ for the forgiveness of your sins, and you shall receive the gift of the Holy Spirit."[7] In other words, you will receive what we have received— the permanent, indwelling presence of God.

And, Bam! Like lightening— the Church was born.

The promise of Jesus to all who belong to Him was powerfully fulfilled on that day. Supernaturally filled. The vessel of Christ's greatest glory was created and empowered. What Paul would later proclaim in his hymn of praise to the Lord was now a reality.

> Now to Him who is able to do exceeding abundantly beyond all that we ask or think, according to the power that works within us, to Him be the glory *in the church* and in Christ Jesus to all generations forever and ever. Amen.[8]

My Church, My Way

"But what about the last question? You know, where Jesus says 'and I will build *My* church.'[9] What part, if any, do *we* play in the building of His church?"

Note His words, "I will build *My* church." That's *My* church— with the *My* referring to Jesus and not to you or me or any other member of His church. He also said that *He* would build *His* church.

Did you catch that? He, Jesus, would build His church. Not us, with our prized programs or our well-thought-out plans. But Jesus, and Jesus alone, would build something that belongs totally to Him.

He would build *His* church.

He would build *His* people.

And He would build it for *His* glory.

Does this sound strange to you? It really shouldn't.

Think about it— Jesus was the One, the *only* One, He commissioned to build *His* church. In His infinite wisdom He decided **not** to entrust that task to anyone else. Good choice. Jesus didn't delegate the responsibility to build His church to subordinates. He didn't dictate to others His desire or hire part-time temps from an employment agency to build His church. Why? Because the outcome, the end result, the finished product, was far too important to Him to leave it to the care of someone else. He, as Lord of the Universe, took personal responsibility to make sure that *His* church was built *His* way— with no margin for error.

The stakes were too high to trust the task to anyone else.

"So," you may ask, "how does Jesus go about building His church?"

Answer: By building people.

"Oh, really?" Yes, really.

If people are truly growing in faith in the Lordship of Jesus Christ and if they're learning to experience Him and taste of the abundant life He promised to each of them, it would stand to reason they would be uncontainably excited about what the Lord was doing in their midst.[10] They would proclaim with Peter and John, unashamed and undeterred, "For we cannot stop speaking about what we have seen and heard."[11]

Frankly, there was no human way you could harness their joy!

Imagine, for a moment, what it must have been like to be able to walk with Peter and John. No matter where they went or who they bumped into in the Wal-Mart parking lot, the message, the joy, just continued to bubble over like a swollen river ready to crest its banks or a dam about to burst. "I just can't help myself," Peter would say, his leathered face breaking into a wide, child-like grin. "I want the whole world to know what Jesus, my Lord and my friend, has done for me! I want to tell *you*! And *you*! I want to tell everybody!"

Or, like Ernest Borgnine said in the classic, 1955, movie, *Marty*, "I can't stop my mouth."

The *If* Factor

Fact is, there's no way you could keep the *church*, the *called-out ones*, silent *if* our times together with the Lord even remotely resembled the times of the first church— powerful, pulsating, filled to the brim with the presence of God, and deeply satisfying to the very core of our being.

But that's a huge *if*.

Granted.

But it's just the way Jesus planned and ordained *church* to be according to the example He gave us in Scripture. Ah, Acts 2, the model, the template, and the prototype of church. Remember? We would all shout from the mountaintops the glory of our Lord *if*...well, uh...*if* we had actually ever experienced, first-hand, what we claim to believe. *If* our knowledge of the things of God were fresh and alive and new like an expensive gift from Saks and not like the worn and tired hand-me-downs from Goodwill with which we're so content to satisfy ourselves. *If* our knowledge of the abundant life Jesus promised was genuine— something we've touched with our own hands and experienced in our own lives.

Like, "We were there! We saw it with our own eyes!"

Or, *if* we just got out of the way and allowed Jesus to build *His* church— *His* way.

"So, if Jesus is to build His *church*, the *called-out ones*— uh, what are we to do? What's our part in all of this?"

Another great question. But wait until you see the answer Jesus has for you!

45

Did Anyone Call for a Disciple?

In Matthew 28, Jesus gave the *church*, the *called-out ones*, the command to go and make "disciples" of all nations.[12]

Note, Jesus said for us to go and make *disciples*. Not converts.

"I don't understand. What's the big deal about that? Aren't they the same thing? What's the difference between a disciple and a convert?"

Much. Mondo Honkin' Much!

Disciples, by definition, are much harder to make and develop than converts. Converts tend to happen relatively quickly. But discipleship is a process that demands time, patience, and a sustained commitment to tutor and help someone become exactly what Jesus called them to be. Hey, let's face it, some of us have been in this discipleship phase of our Christian life for more than 20 years and still haven't got a clue as to what the *new nature* in Christ is all about.[13] Right? Be honest, when it comes to "denying ourselves and picking up our cross daily" we're pretty close to last in line.[14] We might even burn a sick day and not even show up. We all tend to have this nasty habit of taking three steps backwards for every two steps forward and wonder, wide-eyed in disbelief, where the joy of the so-called "abundant life" in Christ is to be found. I mean, who is this "Joy" fellow and where's he hiding? I can't seem to find him anywhere!

Plus, when it comes to making converts, God basically does all the work. Not us.

Think about it. I come up to a guy I meet named Sam and present the truth of the Gospel to him. Maybe I ask him the five standard, Bill Fay, **"Share Jesus Without Fear"** opening questions. [15]

Excuse me, but do you have any kind of spiritual beliefs?

To you, who was Jesus?

Do you think there is a heaven or hell?

If you died, where would you go? If heaven, why?

If what you believe was not true, would you want to know?

Let's assume that Sam's answer to the final question is *yes*— and I'm able to present the truth of the *Good News* to him. I ask Sam if he would like to receive Jesus Christ as his Lord and Savior and Sam says, "Sure."

We pray.

Sam gets saved.

Angels in heaven rejoice.

Great stuff!

Now, look closely at what just happened.

Who's doing all the work?

Is it me, the one who presented the facts of the Gospel to Sam? Do I somehow get the credit or some measure of glory for Sam's salvation? Is the honor all mine? Or does the credit belong to Bill Fay who came up with the questions I used to test Sam's spiritual receptivity to the Gospel?

No, the credit doesn't belong to Bill. And it certainly doesn't belong to me either.

The Holy Spirit, from the foundation of the world, has been working to draw Sam unto Himself.[16] Then what's my part? I'm just privileged to be able to be used by the Lord to present the Gospel to Sam by showing him a couple of Scriptures and asking him a few questions. Sam's salvation is a gift from God, totally undeserved and given because of God's "good pleasure" or the "kind intention of His will."[17] Through the exercise of faith God Himself provides, Sam has come to intimately know, as we affectionately call it, the "saving knowledge of God." He is saved and on his way to heaven.[18]

It's at this point the work of the *church*, the *called-out ones*, really begins.

For it's now the sole responsibility of the *called-out ones*, based on the mandate from its Founder, to turn Sam the convert into Sam the disciple — and that's a difficult, time-consuming, and often frustrating task![19]

Why? For one thing, it takes time.

Lot's of time. Boatloads of time.

It's much like raising a kid from toddlerhood to adulthood, from diapers to diplomas. Jesus' command to the *called-out ones* demands we take someone who knows next to nothing about God, or the Bible, or Christianity, doctrine, the Holy Spirit, the Church, the End Times, prayer, the Blood Atonement and, well, you-name-it, other than the simple fact— "once I was lost, and now I'm saved!"— and somehow ground them deeply in the faith to such an extent they grow to maturity and multiply themselves in others.

Make no mistake, that's a *huge* task!

And every spirit of darkness is working 24/7 to make sure it doesn't happen.

But nevertheless, the mission of the *church* is to do just that— to make disciples.

To go and make *disciples*— or followers of Jesus. No, it's more than just followers. It's to make passionate, sold-out, on-fire, totally committed, disciples of Jesus of all the nations— baptizing them in the name of the Father and the Son and the Holy Spirit and teaching them all that Jesus commanded. "Knowing," as Jesus promised, "that I am with you always, even unto the end of the age."[20]

That's right. We're to be about the task of transforming converts into disciples.

But please understand, we can't accomplish that mission alone.

It's not a matter of mere strategizing or careful planning. And the flawless execution of our particular plan does not in any way guarantee success. No, it requires the involvement of an all-encompassing, all-knowing— omnipotent, omnipresent and omniscient— power beyond anything we can even imagine.

It's solely dependent on the incredible power of the Holy Spirit.

One Final Thought

But what happens when the church refuses to depend on the power of the Holy Spirit? What happens when men and women who have been "bought with a price" determine they know what's best?[21] They know how to build Christ's church? They know how to call all the shots— with or without the blessing of the Lord?

What happens?

The next chapter happens.

We have countless *Tales From the Crypt*.

Real horror stories.

Freddie and Jason and Chuckie all sitting together on the third pew.

Go ahead and turn the page, if you dare, and let me tell you about a few of them.

Each one of them is true.

And each one of them happened to me.

tales from the crypt

"I am determined that my children shall be brought up in
their father's religion, if they can find out what it is."
Charles Lamb (1775-1834)

A Painful Look Over My Shoulder

I was born into a church-going family back in 1955. And I mean
church-*going*— that's an every Sunday, no exception, three-to-thrive, rote
religious, church-*going* family. You know, the kind of real Christian family
that would make Ward and June Cleaver proud.

Come to think of it, I've been going to church for as long as I can
remember.

My dad was the consummate church member— at least to those who
knew him on the outside. He was the willing youth leader who was always
first to volunteer to coach the church basketball team or to sacrifice *his*
Saturday to take the church kids to Dairy Queen for a Blizzard. He served
on almost every committee our church could manage to throw together—
finance, personnel, building and grounds, benevolence, youth— as well as
serving as the coveted Chairman of the Deacons. In fact, when an existing
committee didn't seem to fit the needs of the church, my dad would go the
extra mile and simply invent one to fill the void and then staff it with like-
minded zealots. He was always first to arrive and last to leave knowing that

his devotion to the church was seen as an example to others. If MVP awards were given for church service, my dad would have received the Heisman. Hands down. First ballot.

Every Sunday morning, like clockwork, my dad took on the persona of the warm and inviting, GQ church usher. He would stand at the back of the church, in the foyer, with a stack of folded bulletins tucked neatly under his arm and a broad smile on his face, welcoming each visitor and member with a heartfelt handshake and a pat on the back.

"Frank. Good to see you today. Come on in."

"Bob. How are you and Sarah doing today? And the kids? Great!"

"Ralph! So glad you came. Great havin' you join with us today."

Ah, my dad.

Everyone *loved* him at Dover Shores Baptist Church. Everyone wanted to be like him. And everyone was convinced that "if we just had more people like Bo McCranie at our church, well… we could win this town for Christ!"

But to those of us in the know, to his family, he was a pastor's worst nightmare.

He was a master politician— the Bill Clinton of Dover Shores.

Freddie Kruger in a suit.

Every Sunday we would pack the car, wave to our neighbors, and head off to church. My family would all sit together on a single pew, like cordwood, looking much like Charles Ingles and his Little House on the Prairie family from Walnut Grove. Yep, every Sunday was always the same: Sunday school at 9:45 am and Worship at 11:00 am. Just like it said on the big sign outside.

And so we sat, week after week, all throughout my childhood— listening to the preacher preach, singing hymns from an old, red Baptist Hymnal and waiting patiently for the closing note of the sixth and final stanza of "Just As I Am" to mark the end of another Sunday morning service.

Looking back, I can see this is where spiritual schizophrenia began to raise its ugly head and make itself known to me.

Spiritual Schizophrenia?

"Spiritual schizophrenia? You've got to be kidding!"

50

Oh, believe me, I wish I were.

But sadly, at a very early and impressionable age, I began to experience the Divine Disconnect that the **Love Jesus, Hate Church** religious lifestyle offers. And I saw that hypocritical, spiritual schizophrenia lived out, Sunday after Sunday, by my own father— the award-winning, consummate church member

Let me elaborate a bit for you.

Within the tenets of my church upbringing I was taught, and rightly so, to respect the pastor and to listen to what he had to say. After all, he was the man my father had chosen, or so it seemed at the time, to teach his family the Word of God. We were to follow along in our Bibles, to ponder what the pastor was saying and to diligently take to heart the message we received from the "man of God" each Sunday.

Not much different than any other church, I would presume.

That is, until the fateful ride back home in the family Buick.

Once we shook the pastor's hand on the way out of the church and thanked him for the sermon, the gloves came off. Our car became Madison Square Garden and my father the Undisputed Heavyweight Champion of the Church. My brother and I were buckled in tight with nowhere to run, trapped with ringside seats to the one-sided beating that was about to take place.

Jab: "I didn't like the example the preacher used in his sermon about knowing the will of God. After all, God gave each of us a mind and expects us to use it. I'm going to have to talk with him about that this week."

Jab: "You know, we're going to have to take the pastor down a notch or two at the next deacon's meeting. He just can't always have things his way."

Hook: "And I'm not the only person who feels like that too. There are quite a few of the members... and I mean *tithing* members... who feel the same way."

Jab: "We specifically told him at the last deacon's meeting to let the choir sing before *and* after the offering. Did you see it happen today? No, I didn't think so. He's just ignoring the deacons. Who does he think he is anyway?"

Jab: "I think our pastor has forgotten who pays his salary and signs his checks. Just because he has a seminary degree doesn't mean he can do whatever he wants. No sir! We'll just have to see about that."

Cross: "Maybe... just maybe our church would grow more if we had another pastor. Maybe he's been here too long. Maybe it's time he moved on and we brought in a new face. Hmmm. When we get home I'll make a couple of calls and see how some of the others feel about it. We'll show him who wears the pants in our church."

My dad would continually pound the pastor with rapid-fire combinations and body blows, lefts and rights, never letting him off the ropes. He would tell us, over and over again, about what he disagreed with and how they were going to "straighten out the pastor" at the next committee meeting and that our pastor was "lucky to even have a church like Dover Shores" and "if he didn't wise up he'd be working for McDonalds" and on and on and on.

I think you get the point.

I grew up with this kind of schizophrenic view of religious life. When I was in church I was to honor and respect the pastor as the man of God chosen to proclaim God's Word to us. After all, that's what it said in the Bible. So in church, it was "hands off" the holy man.

But during the rest of the week, his butt was mine!

I could do whatever I wanted with him. I could encourage him or I could tear him down. I could strengthen him or I could tell others how much I disagreed with him and how stupid and wrong he was on everything! And the amazing thing for me is that my father saw nothing inconsistent in this schizophrenic, seesaw type of spiritual pit.

Nothing!

Fast Forward

And I'm amazed that people in church today still view things the same way!

Let me give you just a few examples.

Oh, but first, a bit of a disclaimer.

Disclaimer:

I could easily list, in bullet-point form, literally hundreds of individual cases where the church has been used by people to hurt people and each of these would stand in support of the **Love Jesus**, **Hate Church** tragedy we've been talking about. But in doing so, you would quickly become desensitized to the true nature of these **Love Jesus**, **Hate Church** situations and would probably regress into a self-preservation, "brain freeze" mode and end up scanning rather than reading and reflecting on how we can survive and thrive in today's church culture.

And you would miss the point altogether.

So, as we stated in the last chapter, please understand we are not on a rape, pillage and burn mission against the church. We want, in no way, to drag down what Christ has died for. But we do want to present the truth about church and show, like Christ's message to the church in Ephesus, how "far we have fallen from our first love."[1]

Therefore, each of the situations we will talk about have been experienced, first-hand, by me. That's right, by yours truly. And I have the scars to prove it.[2]

So hang on and let's take a quick journey back into the formative years of my ministry within the church. Unfortunately, you'll probably find much in my past that you've probably experienced yourself. Why? Because there are a lot of Bo McCranies out there!

Who knows, you may even be one yourself.

Jesus: The Real Deal

Before I begin to tell you about my own personal odyssey into the **Love Jesus, Hate Church** commune of spiritual schizophrenia, I must first give honor and praise where it belongs. To my Lord and Savior, the Sovereign Jesus Christ.

I can only begin this chapter by sharing with you how I met the Lord— my personal testimony, if you will. It's my honor to tell you about how the Lord revealed Himself to me.

But even in this, you will see the seeds of **Love Jesus, Hate Church** being sown.

Let's jump right in.

There was an unwritten, time-honored tradition in the Sunday school class I was attending when I was twelve. None of us knew about it as the church year began, but eleven months and three weeks later, we were all keenly aware of it. Simply put, it had become a matter of pride that the teacher of my class never had, at least for the past eight or nine years, any of his students graduate to the next class without making a public profession of Christ. Never! Nada! No way, Jose`.

Rumor was, if you had a tough kid with a bad attitude who just wasn't interested in Jesus, all you would have to do is park him in this teacher's class and it would be the same as if Billy Graham paid him a personal, one-on-one, face-to-face visit. He was as good as saved!

It was big time braggin' rights— and my teacher was battin' a thousand!

And rest assured, this particular year wasn't going to be any different.

As the final Sunday of the church year approached, incredible pressure, almost unbearable pressure, was put upon the ten of us to walk down the aisle as a group and make our profession of faith during the morning worship service. Everyone expected it. The pastor always preached a sermon about it. It was a done deal.

To everyone, that is— except *me*.

As the service that Sunday was drawing to a close and the congregation stood to sing "Just As I Am" for the *six* hundredth time, my father kept giving me this rather forceful nudge with this look on his face that seemed to say, "Uh, what are you waiting for? Let's get on with it, boy. Move!"

But I refused to go. My legs were locked, buried deep in eight yards of cement.

Obediently, like a flock of geese heading south for the winter, my entire Sunday school class, all nine of them, slipped out from the safety of their pews and into the aisle. In single file fashion, like a marching band during halftime, they went down front, shook the pastor's hand, made their profession, were hugged by a bunch of old ladies and then went home.

Everyone— except *me*.

The peer pressure was so thick at home that afternoon, the very air seemed like molasses. In no uncertain terms I was told that Bo McCranie's boy wasn't going to break the tradition. My parents were important people in the church and my refusal to "receive Jesus" with the rest of my class looked like nothing but rebellion to them.

"It's embarrassing," my dad said. "People are going to start wondering what kind of parents we are to raise a son that won't accept Jesus with his friends. What's your problem, boy?"

So the law was set down that Sunday afternoon. My dad was very clear.

"You listen to me, as soon as the first note is played on the organ, you're going to get your butt out of that pew tonight and walk down that aisle and make your profession of faith— even if you have to do it all by yourself. You're going to tell the pastor you wanted to do it this morning with your class but you were scared. Do you understand me? Good. Now put a smile on your face and go make me proud."

And as an impressionable, 12 year-old young man, that's exactly what I did.

The Green Mile

Immediately after the sermon, even before our organist began to bleed "Just As I Am" for now the *seven* hundredth time, I slipped out of my pew and slowly walked, like a condemned prisoner, down the church aisle towards the waiting pastor. He had this huge, omnipotent, "I knew this was going to happen" type of grin on his face. I figured he and my dad must've talked. No big surprise.

It was a perfectly planned, well-meaning, set-up.

Before I could come to a full stop, the pastor reached out and grabbed my hand in his vice-like grip, like we were long-lost kin or something, and pulled me towards him as he began to pepper me with questions. The very same questions I'd heard him ask countless other people when they, too, had completed their pilgrimage from the pew to the pastor. When they had walked their Green Mile. I smiled to myself because I knew all the answers. It was like seeing the math final in advance. Piece of cake!

"Son," he began, raising his voice just enough to make sure most of those in the service that night could hear our conversation. "Do you believe that Jesus Christ is the Son of God?"

"Sure." And I did.

One down. Two to go.

"Do you believe that He died on the cross for your sins, was buried, raised on the third day, is seated at the right hand of the Father and is coming again in glory?" Whew. All in one breath!

"Yes, I do." And again, I did.

"Would you like to go to heaven when you die?"

Well, that's a no-brainer— of course I would. Who wouldn't?

From that point on, everything seemed to slide into high gear. I recited some historical facts about Jesus, prayed a prayer and, Wham! — I instantly became what those of us who suffer from the **Love Jesus**, **Hate Church** form of spiritual schizophrenia affectionately call a "baptized, un-saved, church member."

The rest of the evening was a blur.

People I'd never seen before came by and shook my hand, patted me on the back, messed up my hair and congratulated me for my public profession.

I think just about every old lady in the church hugged me as they each offered a word or two of personal encouragement.

"Good for you, boy. You'll never regret your decision."

"It shor' be good to see young people like you give d'ey lives to the Lord."

"I'll be prayin' for you young man."

"Hey, aren't you Bo McCranie's son?"

Even my Sunday school teacher, with a slick, hard-to-read smirk on his face, congratulated me on my decision and went on to tell me how *proud* he was. You know, even to this day I'm not sure if he was proud of *my* decision for Christ or proud of the fact that *his* record was still intact.

I wonder.

Anyway, right on cue, I was baptized the next Sunday.

It was a real spiritual event for me.

I remember being more concerned about making sure I blew the proper amount of air out of my nose when I went under water than I was with the spiritual significance of being buried in Christ and raised to a newness of life in Him.[3] After all, my primary motivation that evening was to try to avoid embarrassment at all costs!

So from that moment on, at the young age of twelve, my church, my pastor, my friends, my parents and anyone else I had the nerve to voice my doubts to, continually tried to convince me I was saved, changed, born-again, filled with the Holy Spirit, a Christian, yada, yada, yada. I even tried to convince myself of that.

But deep inside, I *knew* I was empty.

I *knew* I was missing something.

I *knew* it didn't take.

I *knew* I was living a lie.

And I *knew* there just had to be more to Christ than this!

ob-la-di, ob-la-da, life goes on...

"Men occasionally stumble over the truth,
but most of them pick themselves up and
hurry off as if nothing ever happened."
Sir Winston Churchill (1878-1967)

Fake It 'Til You Make It!

So what's a young man to do?

For the next 15 years, I tried to fake it until it became real to me. You know, the old multi-level marketing, tried and true, "rah-rah" mantra of "fake it 'til you make it!"

I knew there had to be some people out there who were really experiencing the joy of their life in Christ like the Scriptures promised, but for some reason, they never ran in my circles. All I saw were countless hoards of people who were just as lost as I knew I was— but, like me, refused to admit it. I saw churches slam full of people who took great pains to go through all the right religious motions each Sunday— the patented used-car salesman smiles and the *Praise the Lords* and *Hallelujahs* and *Bless Gods* that marked the beginning of each spoken paragraph like some sort of religious lisp.

But what I didn't see was the genuine joy, passion, or the fervency that comes as a by-product of being changed into the nature of Christ.

Of the indwelling presence of the Holy Spirit.

Of being truly saved.

Nuthin'.

When I studied the Bible, I found it to be a book that was harsh, intolerant, foreign— as if written in some archaic, lost language designed to keep me confused and frustrated. In other words, the Scriptures were simply something that didn't connect with me. On any level.

It was like I was back in high school, studying Shakespeare, trying my best to memorize the lines of *King Lear* or trying to live by the rules of some stupid social club I really didn't want to join in the first place.

Like I cared! Like I gave a flip!

Like it would have any long-term effect, good or bad, on my life!

Ob-La-Di, Ob-La-Da, Life Goes On...

And as it has such a nasty habit of doing, life goes on.

I met my wife and miraculously conned her into marrying me. I'm still not really sure how that happened.

We became quite involved in our local church, more out of habit than anything else. She, as a former preacher's kid, or PK for short, played the church organ for each service and sang in the choir. And I, because of my knowledge of the Bible and my fluent mastery of the language of *churchspeak*, was given the ministry of being the Youth Director and even taught Sunday school. Go figure!

I'm not really sure how that happened either.

Nobody suspected the hypocritical, one-sided life I lived. On Sunday mornings I was the best Christian at our church, at least on the outside. But during the rest of the week, I lived just for me. "I'm as good as anyone else in the church," I reasoned. Everyone marveled at what a Godly young man I appeared to be.

"What a cute couple." Yeah. Just like Bonnie and Clyde.

"We need to get more people like the McCranies to join our church."

I had 'em all fooled— just like my ol' man.

I was becoming the "Bo McCranie" of Decatur Heights Baptist Church.

Me, the consummate church member.

My dad would have been so proud.

So what was my problem?

Simply this: I had a great struggle with the Biblical concept of a Father God. A *huge* struggle! The Bible continually reveals God to us as our Father. Scripture talks about the fact that we can call God our Father, that He is always there for us to take care of us and to protect us like our Father, and that He has our best interest at heart— like our Father. It goes even further in stating God always gives good gifts to His children like a loving Father, and that He will never leave or forsake His children like a Father. In essence, God is presented to us in the Bible as the greatest Father we have or could ever know.[1]

"And that's a good thing?" I would ask, doubting.

Obviously they had never met Bo McCranie.

I had a horrible time trying to understand the "Father" concept of God because I kept superimposing the relationship I had with my own earthly father onto my Heavenly Father. I mean, Bo was the only father I had ever had, the only father to whom I could relate. And if God, as my Heavenly Father, was anything like Bo, my earthly father, well, thanks— but I'll pass.

Your experience may have been different, but my dad was never one who would stand by you when the chips were down or when you really needed him. He always hung you out to dry. Alone. My dad was never without a hidden agenda— a sinister, selfish plan. Therefore, you could never believe anything he said.

Everything about him was suspect. Untrustworthy.

When my dad made a promise, it was only to gain something he wanted or to manipulate the circumstances for his desired outcome. We were all simply expendable pawns in the opening gambit of his master chess game. If what he promised later proved to be a burden— he lied and never delivered.

"Hey," as my brother would later say, "You screwed up. You shouldn't have trusted him."

Ah, vintage Bo McCranie. A spiritual sociopath.

So I grew up believing a father is **not** someone you can trust, **not** someone who would stand by you during hard or difficult times, **not** someone who would ever have your best interest at heart and definitely **not** someone who loved you more than he loved himself. No, a father is someone you could never turn your back on, never trust, was always suspect and would continually strive to impose his greater will on you for his own selfish ends.

Regardless of how it hurts you or those you love.

Needless to say, can you see why I had such a problem with the "Father" concept of God?

Praise God, all that changed when I became a father.

From Christa to Christ

Our first daughter (I have four and one son), Christa, was born when I was 26. I remember it as if it were yesterday, holding her at night, marveling at how wonderful she was and singing to her the impromptu songs I made up on the spot as she would quietly drift off to sleep. I would rock her and rub her back and hold her close for what seemed like hours on end. I couldn't seem to get enough of her. And although she couldn't understand a word I was saying, I found myself each night repeating to her, over and over again, the very vows I committed to her the day she was born.

The vows were simple: "Christa, I love you. You are my child and I am your father. I will *never* lie to you. I will always tell you the truth, no matter what. Christa, I will protect you and gladly give my life for you. Christa, there is nothing in all the world that I would ever do to hurt you. Nothing. You can always count on me— because I am your father."

And little by little, step by step, through my relationship with my own daughter, the Lord began to show me in just a small way what His relationship is like with His children. It slowly began to dawn on me that my Heavenly Father's relationship with me was more like my relationship with my daughter than my dad's relationship had been with me.

One by one, brick by brick, the wall of protection and separation I had built between my Heavenly Father and me began to break away and crumble.

By November of 1983, the clock was winding down.

I'd pretty much had enough. The hypocritical lifestyle I was leading was beginning to disgust me and was quickly coming to an end. I was 28 years old and couldn't live the lie any longer. Didn't *want* to live the lie any longer. I was nauseated by my own life.

My wife and daughter were upstairs sleeping while I was down in the den of our home on the fateful evening God decided to reveal Himself to me. I'd been reading the Bible, aimlessly jumping from one chapter to another, randomly flipping through the pages, praying that something would jump out at me and help me make sense out of what I was feeling or, at the very least, help me find God.

What did I expect? I really didn't know and I really didn't care. But I needed something! Maybe a vision from God or a special verse meant just for me— like a personal message or a confidential briefing. Maybe I was hoping for an angelic hand to write "Mene, Mene, Tekel, Upharsin" on the wall of my den in the same way he did for Belshazzar and Daniel.[2] Who knows?

All I knew was, for the first time in my life, I was hungry enough for *anything* to happen. Anything! But nothing much was going on.

It seemed like it was going to be another long, dull, depressing night.

As I moved from the Old to the New Testament, first to Matthew and then to Micah and back again to Philippians and then on to the Psalms— I felt like a caged tiger pacing back and forth in his cage, waiting for the moment he could escape and break free. I knew there was *Truth* out there. But knowing wasn't enough.

I wanted to experience the *Truth*. I wanted to have a relationship with the *Truth*.

And I didn't care what knowing the *Truth* would cost.

Been There, Done That— Bought the Tee Shirt

I know this may *whack!* your theology a bit, but prior to that evening I'd asked God to come into my life some two to three hundred times or so.

"Really?" Oh yeah, really.

Many times, filled with a genuine longing and deep desire to know God, I would find myself in a revival meeting, making my way down the aisle after the invitation, praying the sinner's prayer with as much faith as I knew how to muster, only to come back empty, discouraged and still lost.

I guess the group pitch approach just didn't take.

Not to be deterred, I then moved to the more one-on-one, hands-on approach to salvation and set up appointments with pastors and evangelists who would faithfully gather around me, lay their hands on me, and pray these long, eloquent, Billy Graham types of prayers until they, too, realized that nothing was going to happen. "Just keep on believing, son. Act like you're saved until it comes to pass."

And now, even the individual pitch didn't work. What's the deal?

I felt like I'd committed the unpardonable sin. That I was un-savable. Beyond redemption. That God really didn't want me. It was like Jesus died for the sins of all humanity "uh, except you, son. You're on your own." Like I was in some really deep *doo-doo* and Jesus wanted no part of me.

Little did I know I had been asking the Lord to come into my life on **MY** terms and not on **HIS** terms. And that's a **HUGE** distinction! Behemoth! Really Big! All I really ever wanted out of a relationship with Christ was the proverbial genie in a bottle— the **Get Out Of Hell Free** card, and little more.

Truth was, I wanted God on *my* terms, to make *my* life better, and to do *my* bidding.

The last thing I wanted, or even understood for that matter, was to have Jesus *as* Lord. Come to think of it, I'm not sure I even understood what the term *Lord* meant.

But Romans 10:9-10 clearly says, "If we confess with our mouth Jesus as LORD, and believe in our hearts that God raised Him from the dead, THEN we shall be saved."[3] For the first time I began to see the connection between Jesus as *Who He Is* and Jesus as *Who We Want Him To Be*.

I laid my Bible down next to me on the sofa and I cried out to the Lord in desperation. And He heard my heartfelt cry. I said, "Lord, I have to know You. I ask You to come into my life on *Your* terms, not on my terms. God, if You're real, and I know that You are— would You please reveal Yourself to me? Would You forgive me of all my sins and make me Yours? I give You my life— all that I am. Please take me, and use me. But Lord, if not, I can't live this way any longer. I'm going to have to walk away. I just can't take this hypocrisy in my life."

Amazingly, I felt an impression to just pick up my Bible and read. So I turned to the Gospel of John, a book that I'd read several times before, and began with the familiar words, "In the beginning was the Word and the Word was with God, and the Word was God."[4] Those words never made much sense to me before that time and they were still pretty vague— like wandering through a thick fog or dimly lit room. There was something about Jesus being the *logos*, the Infinite One, the One who spoke the world into existence. I read about John the Baptist and about Andrew and Peter and Philip and Nathanael. I read on about the miracle at Cana and the cleansing of the Temple at the Passover.

But by the time I made my way into the third chapter of John, God showed up and an incredible thing began to take place right before my eyes.

As I began to read that chapter— one, mind you, that I had read *many* times before— it was as if I was watching the encounter between Jesus and Nicodemus play out before me like a movie or a TV miniseries. I was front row to a Divine encounter. Mine!

The Scriptures, for the first time, became alive to me!

Wow! I can hardly believe this! It was finally happening!

Now I don't want to focus on the details of what happened to the extent that the miracle of salvation, my answer to countless prayers, and the final leg of a 15-year journey to Christ are lost.

But, as best as I can describe it, this is exactly what happened.

Pay Dirt!

It was night and Nicodemus was standing with his back to me, facing Christ. It seemed like I was standing next to Nicodemus, actually a half-step behind, looking over his right shoulder and watching the incredible exchange between this teacher of the Law and the Lord Himself. As Nicodemus spoke to Jesus, the words flowed right out from the pages of Scripture.

"Rabbi," he began, nervously, "We know that You have come from God as a teacher; for no one can do these signs that You do unless God is with him."

Nicodemus began with flattery and Jesus cut directly to the point. Which, I have noticed, is pretty much His style, His MO— or at least the way He deals with me.

"Nicodemus," Jesus began, "Truly, truly, I say to *you*, that unless one (uh, you!) is born again, he (again, you) cannot see the kingdom of God."[5] In other words, "No more small talk. No more beating around the bush. You came to Me to seek truth... OK, then let's talk about the Truth. Let's cut to the chase."

As I was reading the book of John and watching it being played out before me in living, digital, high-definition color, Jesus seemed to look past Nicodemus, to me, and say, "Steve, you also need to be born again."

"How?" I asked before I knew what was happening. "How can a man like me, an adult, re-enter his mother's womb when he is old? How can I be born again? I don't understand."

Jesus smiled and continued, "That which is born of the flesh is flesh. But that which is born of the Spirit is spirit."[6]

Line by line, verse by verse, as I continued to read the dialogue between Nicodemus and Jesus, or between me and Jesus, I discovered the very questions I had were the same ones Nicodemus asked. And the very answers Jesus gave to Nicodemus were the same answers He gave to me.

The Word of God was literally becoming living and active right before me that evening![7]

As I read on, an incredible, eternity-changing thing happened. Before I finished the sixth chapter of John, I had met the Living, Resurrected Christ! God, through His infinite sovereignty, had revealed Himself to me and I knew with utter certainty that my life was different and I belonged to Him.

It had finally happened.

I was saved!

And the joy I experienced cannot adequately be described in words!

63

I remember running upstairs, waking my wife, and saying over and over again with child-like, Christmas morning, awe, "I'm saved! It finally happened! I met Jesus and He made me His child!"

A radical transformation had taken place.

The old man died and the new man— created by God and in His image, was born.

Hallelujah!

i'll never eat at shoney's again

"I won't take my religion from any man who never
works except with his mouth."
Carl Sanburg (1864-1975)

Almost immediately, God called me into the ministry.

Covington Highway Baptist Mission

We were attending White Oak Hills Baptist Church at the time, a traditional, Baptist church in a middle class suburb of Atlanta. The church, or should I say the *pastor*, had a desire to begin a mission church in an unchurched community several miles from where we lived. That summer, a team from Texas came to conduct a survey of the community, assessing needs, building relationships, softening up the soil as it were— a pre-Saddleback sort of thing. I had the opportunity to hang with these guys and, by the end of the summer, we had identified a few key families, and a Bible study was born in the living room of one family's home. Against all odds, I was chosen to lead the study.

Whodathunk, huh?

After a few months, the leadership of White Oak Hills decided it was time to move forward and "occupy the land" as they were fond of saying, and start a mission church. When they began looking for a pastor, I seemed like the logical choice.

So, yours truly became the first (and last) pastor of the Covington Highway Baptist Mission in Stone Mountain, Georgia.

Whodathunk again, huh?

My first church experience was wonderful. Awesome. God did some incredible things in my life and in the lives of those who became our church family and our closest friends. We had about 30 or 40 people attending our service and Bible studies— mostly folks who didn't fit within the traditional church structure. Somehow they missed the train, ran out of money, or simply fell through the cracks of the churches they had attended. These families, no... *our friends*, learned with us the joy of Christian fellowship and worship at CHBM. They were primarily people who loved Jesus but had been hurt by church.

They were wary of church. Afraid.

And really had no other place to go.

No other place to fit in.

We had a couple that were spiritually mentoring us at the Mission and overseeing the work— much like a Paul to young Timothy. Bill and Naomi Hunke were former missionaries and had worked extensively with the local Baptist Ministerial Association. Needless to say, when I stood to preach my first sermon at the Covington Highway Baptist Mission, I learned, or was beginning to learn, what it was like to be a pastor. I began to experience the joy of being around other men of God who were just as sold out to Jesus as I believed I was.

I was also beginning to learn how naive I was to the ways of church. But all that was soon to change. I was about to take a graduate level crash course on **Church: American Style**.

I'll Never Eat At Shoney's Again!

Six or seven months into my first pastorate, Bill Hunke encouraged me to attend the local Baptist Association meeting. Bill lovingly lectured me and said, "Steve, you know the more logs that are thrown into a fire, the longer and brighter that fire will burn. Left alone, a single log will soon burn itself out."

Meaning: "You *need* to be around these other Baptist pastors. You might learn something from them and they might learn something from you."

Bill was right. I *did* learn quite a bit from these other Baptist pastors.

And I learned it very early in my ministry. Painfully early.

The infamous Baptist Association Meeting was a gathering of about 40 or so of the pastors of some of the largest Baptist churches in our area. Every month, right after the breakfast rush cleared out, these pastors would all come together in a private room at the back of our neighborhood Shoney's. The setting was informal and loosely formatted, by design. This was to help "facilitate spiritual bonding and mutual dialogue between local Baptist pastors," I was later told by the Director of Missions. I think he must have been reciting the Association's Mission Statement or something.

Anyway, it seemed like a pretty good idea to me at the time.

I don't know what I expected on that Tuesday morning as I made my way into the private dining area of the nearly deserted Shoney's. I guess I envisioned this meeting to be something significant, something spiritual— something on the same level as being in the upper room where men of God would gather together to worship, to encourage each other and to strategize on how they could collectively fulfill the Great Commission.

Actually, it turned out to be more like a lynch mob or one of those National Geographic specials we've all seen where a pack of snarling, drooling, hungry wolves descends on a defenseless herd of sheep, circling, allowing no escape— and then one by one savagely picks off and devours the weakest among the flock.

But wait, I'm jumping ahead.

We all sat at a long table, drank coffee and made small talk. The meeting was moderated by the local Director of Missions, a DOM for short, and there was ample time for some to share about what was working or not working in their churches, reports on how many they were "runnin' in Sunday school" or how God was blessing their respective ministries.

Typical pastor *brag* sort of stuff.

To be honest, I felt awed and intimidated as I sat there with all these experienced, full-time, seminary educated, respected, veteran pastors. I was still a ministry rookie and these guys were seasoned veterans. They'd made it to the *big time* and I was still playing minor league ball. I was this young, "new kid on the block" pastor of a little mission church sitting at the table with pastors who had more babies in their nursery than I had members in my church. Some of these guys were called into the vocational ministry even before I was born.

Anyway, I was excited about the opportunity to be with them. Proud just to be able to associate with a group of men like them. So I took Bill Hunke's advice and sat back, listened intently, took mental notes and tried to glean whatever pearls of wisdom I could from their conversation.

After the small talk and the second cup of coffee, the moderator stood up and said, "Before we begin, is there any old business we need to discuss?"

Like the other pastors, I looked around to see if anyone had something to say.

The gentleman sitting directly across the table from me was the pastor of a large Baptist church located about three miles from our church. They'd just completed a two year building program and now boasted of a new, multi-million dollar, state-of-the-art worship facility. I'd never seen the inside of the building, but the outside looked pretty impressive.

To my surprise, this pastor stood and said, "Yes, there *is* some old business. If you remember there was an important issue we talked about last month that was never resolved. I would like to discuss it again."

All attention focused on him, waiting for him to continue. The room seemed to grow strangely quiet.

And there I was, sitting right across from this respected pastor, with a ringside seat to this all-important, unresolved, spiritual matter. I remember thinking how blessed I was to be at Shoney's on that Tuesday morning. I remember thinking how I was going to thank Bill Hunke, maybe even take him out to lunch, for insisting I come to this meeting. I felt like young Timothy learning from an Apostle Paul.

"This is sooooo cool," I said to myself.

The Director of Missions sighed, rolled his eyes, and reluctantly acknowledged the question.

"Ok, Frank. Let's talk about it *one* more time."

And then the unthinkable happened.

Balloon burst.

Parade rained on.

Pet dog died.

Hindenburg crashed.

Turning his gaze directly towards me, his eyes filled with something *other* than love and compassion, the pastor, Frank, pointed his chubby, ringed finger in my face and said, "I want to know why this guy's church is even in existence. Like I said last month, I want it gone! It doesn't belong in *my* area. I don't want his church in *my* back yard."

I was shocked, dumbfounded, and literally speechless.

Everything seemed to slow down. I felt like the very essence of my being had been violated. I had no idea what was going on. I was clueless. It was almost like the old, reoccurring college nightmare where everybody else in the class had read the answers to the questions, and I walked in late and didn't even know we were taking a test!

I was totally unprepared for what had just taken place. Caught with my pants down!

I remember stammering something to the effect of, "Uh, what are you talking about?" as I looked up and down the table, surveying each face, trying desperately to see if I was the *only* one in the dark.

Heated discussion broke out everywhere, like semi-automatic gunfire. Everyone was talking at once. It sounded like I was caught in the middle of a bunch of floor traders on the NYSE.

There were some that agreed with *Frank the Pastor* and defended his actions.[1]

"Frank's right, the church was planted without proper authorization."

"There wasn't an Associational vote on it, was there? I don't ever remember voting for a new church. Do you?"

"If we're going to have rules, then we need to follow them. I wouldn't want the Association planting a start-up church in my backyard. Would you?"

A few other people, those who *didn't* have churches near mine, argued the other side of the issue.

"If this guy's doing a good work in his church, let's just leave him alone. We need to encourage each other, not tear each other down."

"I'm sorry this had to happen, young man. Frank is... well,...Frank is Frank. He's a good guy that gets a little strange sometimes. What more can I say?"

I finally remember a man sitting next to me, a fit guy with gray hair in his mid-fifties, reaching out and putting his arm around my shoulder and saying to them, "Why don't we just leave this young pastor alone and let him go about doing God's work?"

The rest of the meeting was a blur. I don't know *how*, or *if*, anything was resolved.

Welcome to **Church: American Style**.

I later found out the pastor of White Oak Hills was bucking for a position with the Southern Baptist Convention as some sort of denominational representative— which is like a contract teacher with tenure. The only way you could lose your job was to kill somebody— with an ax. The unwritten requirement for advancement and a quick trip up the corporate ladder into the bureaucracy of the SBC was to show on your resume that your church was active in establishing mission churches.

Ah, plot thickens.

So without the proper blessings from the other churches in the area, the pastor of White Oak Hills, in collusion with the Director of Missions, decided to plant a church for purely selfish motives— for a job promotion. Ugh! And I became pastor of that church. The members of the congregation of the Covington Highway Baptist Mission were, in essence, nothing more than expendable pawns in a political chess game that caused ripples among the ecclesiastical community.

Well, I had my first taste of organized church and it was real bitter. In fact, it sucked!

That very day I made a vow and foolishly never kept to it. I vowed to myself that I would never again attend a denominational meeting of any sort and for any reason, but would instead focus my life on *real* ministry to *real* people.

But unfortunately, the lesson I just shared with you I had to learn over and over again.

Are you beginning to see how people can **Love Jesus** and **Hate Church**?

embittered rage of the spirit

"We do not want churches because they will
teach us to quarrel about God."
Chief Joseph (1840-1904), *Nez Perce Indian Tribe*

I really don't know how to begin this.

You see, lately I've been experiencing something deep in my own spirit that, at first, I didn't think was very healthy. And that bothered me. Bothered me a lot. But now I'm not so sure. I'm not so sure that what I was experiencing in my spirit wasn't actually quite healthy after all. Maybe it was *very* healthy. I guess time will tell.

Let me elaborate.

Embittered Rage of the Spirit

Face it, that title doesn't really sound like anything we've ever been taught in Sunday school, does it? It sounds somewhat polarizing. Intrinsically confrontational. Not very tolerant. Especially when you consider the glut, the self-absorbed slew of those who pathologically try to soft sell the Truth. You know, the pathetic peddlers of the "ever tolerant" who thrive in our mushy atmosphere of the "God is *only* love" sentiment that marks the values and identifies the dominant, prevailing character of the church times in which we find ourselves today.

Love and Rage— culturally defined as two seemingly incompatible and conflicting emotions. Totally inconsistent with our understanding of the Christian life.

Right?

Well, now I'm not so sure.

Embittered Rage of the Spirit

By the way, the phrase comes from a Biblical passage found in the third chapter of the writings of Ezekiel. Just in case you were wondering.

Embittered Rage of the Spirit

I've found myself, especially over the last couple of years, increasingly powerless to be able to casually blow things off the way I used to. I find it hard, almost impossible, to pretend they really don't bother me. To wear the fake church face, perfect the façade and attempt to act as if I really don't care. To hypocritically try to deny what I'm feeling. It's like the hinge that operates my "Hey, I don't care…" shoulder shrugger mechanism is rusty and desperately needs oil from the Tin Man's oil can.

It's stuck, won't budge, and doesn't work for me the way it used to.

I've wondered countless times why I can't just "live and let live" or why the water doesn't run off "this ol' duck's back" anymore? Why do things bother me like they do? Why do I let them get under my skin?

What's wrong with me?

Have I changed? Maybe.

I've tried to blame this apparent change on my age or maybe on the fact I'm trying to lose weight. It's a well-documented fact, by the way, that a steady diet of diets will quickly erode your ability to passively sit back and ignore personal irritants. Maybe that's it. Diets, if left undiagnosed and untreated, can turn even the most docile person into a personal irritant.

Maybe I'm just becoming a personal irritant.

I've also pointed the accusing finger to the fact that I'm the father of five kids and the pastor of a small church. Hey, don't laugh. We're talking about the Addams Family here!

Anyway, over the years I've tried to blame it on lots of different things. But the fact is, I've just not been able to casually shrug my shoulders and blow things off the way I have in the past. The tried-and-true seminary taught defense mechanism designed to keep me insulated from involvement and inevitable hurt just doesn't seem to work anymore.

At this point, hopefully, you've realized that I don't get "my panties twisted in a wad" by every petty thing that comes my way or by every single person that crosses my path. I believe the fact that you've read this far in this book indicates you must have determined I'm not some old, bitter, cantankerous pastor using a sawed-off, double-barreled, scattergun of cynicism to wound with buckshot everyone who innocently strays into my range.

It's not that way at all.

Actually, there's *only* one specific thing, or one specific *category* of things that get under my skin. But this one category enrages me.

Hits my hot button.

Pushes me right up to the edge, to the point of no return— and then pushes again.

Only harder.

This category has to do with what I like to call the genetic hypocrisy and generational apathy present in the church of Christ today. The *lie* we lamely confuse with the abundant life. The deception we've warmly embraced as the defining characteristic of our spiritual existence. The firmly entrenched, sincerely held mindset that is literally woven into the core fabrics of our Biblical understanding.

It has become our lukewarm, Laodicean heritage.

I get so hot when I hear stories— and there are *boatloads* of them circulating today— about Christians acting like non-Christians and non-Christians acting better than Christians, that I want to stand in front of the Wal-Mart Superstore and shout to anyone who will listen, "Enough! Please don't think Jesus is like your pastor or your church or any other Christian you know. He's not! He's not like us. We are to be like Him, but we've failed—and failed miserably!"

Do you know why we've failed so miserably?

Because, as Jesus said, we "love the darkness more than the light." Why? "Because our deeds are evil."[1]

My attitude used to be more like, "Ah, that's just who they are. Those poor, sad Christians. After all, nobody's perfect. They're just human."

But not anymore.

Now it's to the point where the blatant hypocrisy of the church demands a response.

Have It Your Way!

For example, I'm sitting at Burger King the other day, minding my own business, drinking my Diet Coke and writing the chapter you're now reading. Sliding into the booth behind me are these two moderately overweight women, both in their mid-forties, who begin to talk about their church. Quite *loudly*, I might add. As if they were the only two in the restaurant. At first I tried to ignore the annoying, rising chatter of their conversation. But the growing, emotional intensity I heard in their voices was beginning to overpower my dogged desire to concentrate. Gradually, like a moth drawn to a porch light, I found myself increasingly sucked into their conversation.

"And I don't know why *she* thinks *she* gets to sing the solo," the lady with an indignant tone in her voice complained, dramatically punctuating each "*she*" with a slur of sarcasm. "*She* sang lead last year and it's time someone else had a turn."

Pause.

First for dramatic effect— and then for the French fries to cool.

"Just who does *she* think *she* is?"

"Did you see the dress *she* wore Sunday?" the one sitting back to back to me with a nasal whine in her voice, replied. "Wonder who *she* was trying to impress with that outfit?"

"All I know is that as soon as I get back home I'm going to start making some calls and put a stop to all of this," replied indignant.

"Who you gonna call?" asked the whiney one.

"Some of the other members of the choir feel just like I do. We were talking about it Sunday night after practice. And they don't like the way the new choir director is playing favorites. There have been some of us who have sung in the choir for many years... long before we hired the director. We'll just see who'll sing lead in this year's Easter Cantata. We'll just see."

And on and on and on this crap went. Public. Out in the open. In the booth of Burger King, for crying out loud! Within the earshot of dozens of people who were all forced to listen, just like me, to a blow-by-blow, no-holds-barred, ring-side description of a petty dispute regarding who would get to stand center stage in a church production designed to honor the greatest act of humility ever known to man— the death and resurrection of the Sinless One.

Talk about missing the point!

So, I'm sitting there in my own booth, with front row seats to this living testimony of the *non*-changing power of Christ and the *not-so*-abundant life, feeling the edges of my ears beginning to turn red and my blood pressure rapidly rising. Instead of taking the easy and tolerant way out— shrugging my shoulders in apathy, shaking my head in disgust and turning back to mind "my own business"— I wanted to jump up and plant myself in front of their faces and shout, "Shut up! I mean, keep your mouths shut! Don't you realize there are people around here who don't know Christ, and your testimony about Him sucks. Big time! Boy, I bet all the people who've been listening to you shoot your mouth off can't wait to have the love and joy that you've shown them you have right now. Don't you realize that it's not all about *you*? It's all about *Him*. Hey, act like you belong to Him or just keep your mouth shut!"

Normally I'd just blow it off.
But not anymore. I just can't.
This defaming of Jesus by those who claim to be His *demands* a response.

I hear stories all the time, and I'm sure you do too, about pastors who do things they shouldn't be doing, manipulating and lying to congregations to achieve their own selfish ends. I am privy to tales of deacons who are power hungry, of the moral decay within the ranks of Christianity and of apathy run amuck within the house of the Lord. I've heard it all— and it sickens me.
Does it sicken you?

I find myself violating a fundamental law of our culture by becoming less and less tolerant towards people who claim to be Christians and yet don't live like it. Oh yes, the blind toleration of sin and apathy is *not* a Biblical virtue. Regardless of what you've heard preached from pulpits, Sunday after Sunday, or seen, channel after channel, on religious TV, across our nation.
Truth is, "If we claim to walk in the light yet live in darkness, we are a liar and the truth is not in us."[2] That's not just my opinion. That's the Holy Spirit speaking through the pen of John.
Go ahead. Read it for yourself.

God Speaks in the Strangest Places

I'm sitting at Burger King, terribly troubled, asking the Lord about all this.
"What's going on with me, Lord? Am I becoming an old, angry guy with a chip on his shoulder? Why do I feel this way? Is something changing inside of me? What's happening here?"

And then it happened.

The Lord clearly spoke to me in the booth of a Burger King that day and told me that the answers to my questions are found in the book of Ezekiel.

"Ezekiel?" I asked. "Are You sure? Did I hear You right?"

Oh yeah, I heard Him right.

Let's be honest, you only read Ezekiel if you want to talk about the valley of dry bones or the resurgence of Israel or for some of the other end-time, prophetic stuff. It's not a book of the Bible that naturally lends itself to inspirational reading. On a cold December evening, as you sit warm and cozy in front of a crackling fire sipping hot cider, you usually don't reach for the book of Ezekiel.

Somehow it just doesn't seem to fit the occasion— seems out of place.

Anyway, I quickly turned to the book of Ezekiel and began to read the first chapter and— **WOW!**

The answer to *everything* that was going on in me, to *everything* I was feeling and to *everything* I was experiencing was found within the first few pages of Ezekiel.

In black and white.

Right before my eyes.

How could I have not seen it before?

The answer to, the reason for, and the source of everything I was struggling with came clearly through the pen of Ezekiel. It all had to do with Ezekiel's call and commission into the ministry of the Lord.

It was utterly amazing!

Let me ask you, are you frustrated with what you see shamelessly masqueraded as Christianity in the church today?

Are you tired of the counterfeit?

Like the Coke commercial, do you long for the "Real Thing"? The genuine stuff? The real deal?

If so, keep reading and we'll discover together what the Lord has to say today to His children, *the church*, through the book of Ezekiel.

we got lotta mo!

"I like your Christ, I do not like your Christians.
Your Christians are so unlike your Christ."
Mohandas Gandhi (1869–1948)

Ezekiel Who?

If you take the time, you'll discover in the first chapter of Ezekiel that God gives him an incredible glimpse, a taste, a free sample of what life is like in the heavenlies. It's almost as if, just for an instant, the Almighty pulls back the curtains of this world and lets Ezekiel bask in the indescribable light of the world to come. Needless to say, it permanently changed and realigned the focus of Ezekiel's life from that moment on.

I know you've read it all before (or, at least you should have), so we'll dispense with the formalities and dive right into the text.

Chapter One

In this first chapter, Ezekiel describes his encounter with the Lord in terms of a huge, awesome storm, and as "a great cloud with fire flashing forth continually and a bright light around it, and in its midst something like glowing metal in the midst of the fire."[1] Then, from the center of the storm, in a manner reminiscent of John on the Isle of Patmos, Ezekiel attempts to describe the four living beings that emerged from the tempest. They each had human form, uh...*somewhat*— each with four faces and four wings, and their feet resembled calves' feet. There were also four sets of human hands under each of the four wings. Oh, "As for the form of their faces, each had the face of a man, all four had the face of a lion on the right and a bull on the left, and all four had the face of an eagle."[2]

Do you see what's happening here?

This was an incredible vision God was giving to Ezekiel— not unlike the visions He also gave John in Revelation 4 or Isaiah in Isaiah 6.

It was an awesome display *of* God— *from* God.

God was giving Ezekiel a glimpse of who He is.

The chapter goes on to describe, in amazing clarity and detail, the famed "wheel within a wheel" and concludes with Ezekiel's telling about the vision of divine glory that he was blessed to experience.[3] This latter part, his description of Divine Glory— is the pinnacle, the crescendo, the crowning moment— pretty much the icing on the cake of his celestial visitation.

I think it's best to let Ezekiel describe it in his own words:

> "Then I noticed from the appearance of His loins and upward something like glowing metal that looked like fire all around within it, and from the appearance of His loins and downward I saw something like fire; and there was a radiance around Him. As the appearance of the rainbow in the clouds on a rainy day, so was the appearance of the surrounding radiance. Such was the appearance of the likeness of the glory of the LORD. And when I saw it, I fell on my face and heard a voice speaking."[4]

Needless to say, Ezekiel was overwhelmed and awed by this indescribable vision and encounter with the Lord.

In essence, Ezekiel received a first-hand vision of what the Lord was really like. Pretty much the same vision Paul had on the Damascus road. The same vision you and I had when we received Jesus Christ as our Lord and Savior. Maybe it's not as dramatic as falling off a donkey and being blinded for three days like Paul, but it was still the same "out of darkness, into light" experience.[5]

Now, Chapter Two...

The first verse of chapter two begins with the account of God immediately calling Ezekiel into the ministry. "Then He said, 'Son of man, stand on your feet that I may speak to you.' And He spoke to me, and as He spoke to me the Spirit entered me."[6]

Did you notice what I noticed?

Scripture clearly states that the Spirit entered Ezekiel.

The Spirit empowered him, baptized him, and now resided within him. Ezekiel had what we would call a genuine Acts 2 type of encounter with the Third Person of the Trinity. What Ezekiel experienced in chapter two is exactly what you and I experienced in our own life the very day we got saved— at the very instant we became justified in the sight of God by virtue of the blood of Jesus. The Holy Spirit that now possessed Ezekiel, that now inhabited and empowered Ezekiel, is the *same* Holy Spirit that now resides in us.

Seems we're not as far removed from the life of a prophet as we'd like to think.

Anyway, look what happened next.

> "The Spirit came to me and set me on my feet and I heard Him speaking to me. Then He said to me, 'Son of man, I'm sending you to the sons of Israel, to your *own* people, to a rebellious people who have rebelled against Me. They and their fathers have transgressed against Me to this very day. I am sending you to them who are stubborn and obstinate children of Mine and you shall say to them, 'Thus sayeth the Lord God.' As for them, whether they listen or not, they will know that a prophet has been among them and a man of God stands in their midst.'"[7]

Don't miss this. It's real important.

Read it again, carefully.

God's commission to Ezekiel, His command to His servant, was to send him into the midst of his *own* people, to interact with his *own* countrymen and to boldly proclaim the Word of the Lord to those with whom he had all things in common. He was called by his Lord to faithfully proclaim undiluted truth to those both deceived and deluded with the lie.

Literally, Ezekiel was to be the *salt and light* that Jesus, centuries later, would passionately speak about.[8]

Throughout the pages of the book of Ezekiel you'll find God continually instructing Ezekiel that he is to speak *only* what he hears from the Father— and nothing more. God said to Ezekiel, "You shall say to them, 'Thus says the Lord God.' Whether they listen or not really doesn't matter because they're obstinate and they're stubborn and they want their own way. Nevertheless, you speak My Word and they will know that there's a prophet, a man of God in the house. They will know that My Spirit lives in somebody and that he speaks for Me."[9]

Or, as the old Baptist preacher would paraphrase, "Hey, Zeke, yo' da man fo da day. Go fer it!"

I'm telling you, what God commanded Ezekiel to do in his day is the same mandate that Jesus gives to each one of us in our day. We are to make disciples of all nations.[10] We are to speak the truth with all diligence. And, whether they listen to us or not, we must persevere and tell them what we have heard from the Father. Why? Because, to quote Peter and John, "We can't help but to speak and teach what we have seen and heard."[11] After all, Jesus said all authority and all power is given unto Him on earth and He promised to be with us always, even unto the end of the age. "Therefore go and make disciples of all nations."[12]

I can't find a way to water this command down. Can you?

Didn't think so.

It just doesn't seem to get any clearer to the church than this.

The Divine Commission

Then chapter three begins, for the lack of a better term, with the divine commissioning of Ezekiel to the task God had set before him. By the way, as a sidebar of sorts, do you know the difference between Ezekiel's call and commissioning and the particulars of *your* personal call into the work of the Lord?

Not much.

Think about it, God sent Ezekiel to speak His Word to the sons of Israel and He has commanded us to "make disciples of all nations."[13] He equipped and empowered Ezekiel with the Holy Spirit just like He has empowered and equipped you and I— the church, the *called-out ones*— with the same Spirit. And, He has given each of us the same charge, the same decree that He gave to Ezekiel.

"And what's that charge?" you ask.

Namely, to speak God's word to God's people.

"If they listen, great!" God was telling Ezekiel in his day. "But even if they don't listen, you are to speak My words to them." Over and over in the writings of Ezekiel we see God saying, "I will open your mouth and I will close your mouth. I will make your tongue cleave to the roof of your mouth so that you can't even talk until I'm ready to loosen it, because I only want you to speak the words that come from Me. Not *your* opinions, not *your* desires, and not *your* words. I want you to go to a rebellious people who have rebelled against Me, and transgressed against Me, and are stubborn and obstinate and tell them My words. Tell them what I have told you to tell them and nothing more. Got it? Good. Now, go!"[14] Wow!

Every time I read this I realize there's nothing all that different about Ezekiel and those He calls and indwells today.

Nothing save, maybe— passion and obedience. Ouch.

Is There Anything More?

As Mr. T would say, "We got lotta mo!"

Check out the exchange between God and Ezekiel.

> "Go to the house of Israel and speak to them, for you are not being sent to a people that are of unintelligible speech or difficult language, but unto the house of Israel."[15]

It was like God was saying, "Good grief, Ezekiel, I'm not sending you somewhere where you'll be a stranger. Look, you've got it easy. You don't have to go through five years of language studies, earns a seminary degree or learn about the various nuances of a different culture to be My mouthpiece. I'm simply asking you to be a witness to your *own* people, to your family, neighbors and friends. I'm sending you to a people that know your language and understand the oracles of God— or at least they should. All you have to do is your job. Just do your job."

Do your job.

> "Nor many people of unintelligible speech or difficult language, whose words you cannot understand. But I have sent you to them who *should* listen to you. Yet

81

the house of Israel will not be willing to listen to you
since they are not willing to listen to Me. Surely the
whole house of Israel is stubborn and obstinate."[16]

Sounds just like today, doesn't it?

Only, instead of the sons of Israel we have the mission field of the
stubborn and obstinate church. The mission field made up of those who
claim to love God but live like they don't.

"But," you may be asking yourself, "what if I go and I tell them over
and over again and they keep telling me, *no*. Can I quit? Can I give up? I
mean, maybe it's not really worth it."

Really? Read on.

"Behold I have made your face as hard as their faces
and your forehead as hard as their foreheads, like
emory, harder than flint, I have made your forehead.
So do not be afraid or dismayed before them, though
they are a rebellious house. Moreover, He said to me,
'Son of man, take into your heart all My words which
I shall speak to you and listen closely and go to the
exiles, to the son of your people, and speak to them
and tell them, whether they listen or not, thus sayeth
the Lord God.'"[17]

If that's not the Great Commission in Old Testament language, then I
don't know what is.

Embittered in the Rage of the Spirit!

"And then the Spirit lifted me up," Ezekiel records, "and I heard a great
rumbling sound behind me. And I heard this 'blessed be the glory of the
Lord in His place.' And I heard the sound of the wings of the living beings
touching one another and the sounds of the wheels beside them, even a great
rumbling sound. So the Spirit lifted me up and took me away. And I went
embittered in the rage of my spirit. And the hand of the Lord was strong
upon me."[18]

Did you catch that?

Ezekiel was called and commissioned by God to proclaim to a
stubborn, obstinate and thickheaded people the undiluted "Thus saith the

Lord…" from the very lips of God. And Scripture says he went "*embittered in the rage of his spirit*."[19]

Did you ever wonder why?

That seems like a strange response to a Divine mandate.

"*Embittered in the rage of his spirit*."

I wonder what Ezekiel must have been feeling?

I Know *Exactly* How You Feel

Now I know. I know *exactly* what Ezekiel was feeling.

He was feeling exactly what I was feeling at Burger King that day as I was forced to listen while two whining, lukewarm, thumb-sucking, nauseating church members trashed the glory of God by their public complaining and self-absorbed jealously. Uh, remember *indignant* and *whiney* from the last chapter?

Exactly what I feel every time I hear one so-called "Believer" viciously gossip about another with the intention of tearing one down to build another up.

Exactly what I feel when elders, deacons or church members talk about their pastors in derogatory terms designed to cast derision and disrespect under the false guise of being spiritual.

Exactly what I feel when I see members in a church pouting or frowning or refusing to sing praise to their God because they don't like the music, the tempo, the instruments, the style or the person leading in worship.

Exactly what I feel when I hear of church splits, moral failures, financial irregularities, or obscene worldliness among those for whom Christ suffered and died.

Those He *died* for! Arrgh!

It is precisely what I've been feeling— pure, unharnesed rage— in my own spirit the past several years as I looked at the pathetic, weak, anemic condition of the church.

It's exactly what I am feeling now.

No wonder Jesus wanted to vomit us out of His mouth![20]

Face it, when Ezekiel received his command, his mandate, and his life's message from God, he didn't go to the children of Israel with a tolerant, "I want to please everybody" attitude like we do today. He didn't purposely soft sell the message for the sake of the listener's poor, pitiful, fragile feelings. He didn't degrade and devalue the very words from God for the sake of personal popularity.

Ezekiel knew they were going to get offended, and he didn't care.

No, Ezekiel was enraged— and he went to them enraged.
Why? Why was Ezekiel so enraged?

He was enraged at the pathetic condition of their lives.
He was enraged with their sin, their apathy and their total ambivalence to the Lord.

He refused to make excuses for their actions, like we are so fond of doing today, by patronizingly saying, "God hates the sin, but He *loves* the sinner."

As if that statement somehow negates the need for the blood of Christ and grants us divine permission to sin. Something akin to our infamous Bumper Sticker Theology that states, **Christians Aren't Perfect, Just Forgiven.**[21]

Instead, Ezekiel was enraged at what he saw in the lives of God's people— and it filled him with righteous anger.

He cut them no slack.

He took no prisoners.

These were, after all, God's people. These were the very people who claimed to know Him, to love Him, and to have a relationship with Him. These were the very ones He redeemed, those "He carried forth on eagles wings."[22]

They were His children, beloved by Him. He gave them His Word, His comfort and His protection. He spoke to them, revealed His will to them and redeemed them with His mighty hand.

Do you know how His children honored and expressed their eternal gratitude for the priceless gift they had received from God?

They ignored His mercy and grace and coldheartedly blew him off.

Like it was no big deal.

Like it was nothing to them.

Like *He* was nothing to them.

They didn't care.

They were *too* tied up, *too* engrossed, *too* enamored, *too* consumed with their own selfish wants and indulgent desires to give a flip about anyone else— including God!

When Ezekiel compared what he'd just seen and heard in the heavens, what he'd experienced first-hand of the glory of the Lord— with the callous, abject disrespect displayed by the very objects of God's love, the children of the Father, he was so blind with anger at the hypocrisy of God's people that he went away embittered, enraged in his spirit.

Not to be too blunt, but Ezekiel was royally pissed-off.

And, quite honestly, so am I.

Are you? And if not, *why* not?

Where Do We Go From Here?

The reason Ezekiel was enraged was because those who rejected the Lord, those who rejected His message, were the very ones the Father deeply loved. They were the ones who should have known better. They were the ones whose rejection hurt the most.

They were, in today's vernacular, the *Church*. **The Well-Oiled Machine**.

But they'd left their first love to feast at the table of apathy.[23]

And since it pissed-off Ezekiel— then I guess it's OK for me to be pissed-off too.

How about you?

What are you prepared to do about it?

Does the degrading of the sacrifice of Christ demand a response? If so, does it demand that response from *you*?

"That's pretty hard stuff. Intense. I don't know if it's my responsibility to tell others what God says in His Word. After all, that's the preacher's job."

Watchman on the Wall Stuff

True. It's the responsibility of the preacher to proclaim the Word of the Lord.

But, it's not his responsibility *alone*.

A couple of verses later, and repeated several times throughout the book, God told Ezekiel that He had appointed him as a "watchman over the house of Israel."[24]

I know you've probably heard sermons on these passages before. If you've been in church for any length of time, well…you should have. So, let me bring this chapter to a close by telling you what the "watchman on the wall" passages are all about.

They basically state that *if* there is a wicked man who is going along in his wickedness and you warn him and you say, "Man, what you're doing is against God's Word. You need to repent and change. Turn or burn!"— you have faithfully fulfilled your duty to him as a messenger of God. *If* he ignores your warning, blows you off, flips you the finger and continues in his wickedness, the Scriptures clearly state he will die in his sin but God will not hold you accountable for his blood.[25] Why?

Because you did your job.

You told him the truth.

You communicated God's Word to him and he chose not to obey.

And the consequences for his actions are now his responsibility.

On the other hand, *if* a wicked man is caught up in his wickedness and turns and repents when confronted with the Word of the Lord— then his subsequent deliverance, his transformation and his very salvation bring glory to the Lord. You, in turn, please Him by your obedience. Why?

Because, once again, you've done your job.

If, however, that same man finds himself being drawn away and pulled into his wickedness and you just clap your hand over your mouth, look away and refuse to say anything— Scripture warns that this man will suffer the consequences of his own sins and die, but God will rightly require his blood at your hands.

"Am I my brother's keeper?" you, like Cain, may ask.[26]

Absolutely! That's why God called us a family!

"But, that's not very tolerant. People may get offended. If I talked to people like Ezekiel did they would...well...er...they might go to another church."

Uh, and the point is?

The Bottom Line

We all fall into one of two groups.

Group one is made up of those who are called by His name and serve as His watchmen, those who faithfully fulfill the divine mandate from our Lord to speak the truth in love and tell the world about the saving grace of our Lord Jesus Christ.[27]

For you, Ezekiel would say, "Get enraged! Get involved! Get mad at the ease of sin and the apathy of the church and preach the Word of God with all boldness. Let them know, whether they heed your warnings or not, that there's a man of God in the house."

In other words, "Do your job!"

86

Then, there's the other group. Those who received the same mandate from the Lord as the first group, but...

I'll let Jesus speak in the place of Ezekiel.

> "I know your deeds, that you are neither cold nor hot; I wish that you were cold or hot. So because you are lukewarm, and neither hot nor cold, I will *spit* (uh, that's projectile vomit) you out of My mouth. (Why?) Because you say, 'I am rich, and have become wealthy, and have need of nothing,' and you do not know that you are wretched and miserable and poor and blind and naked. I advise you to buy from Me gold refined by fire so that you may become rich, and white garments so that you may clothe yourself, and that the shame of your nakedness will not be revealed; and eye salve to anoint your eyes so that you may see. Those whom I love, I reprove and discipline; therefore be zealous and repent."[28]

Are you beginning to see how easy it is to **Love Jesus** and **Hate Church**?

And, are you beginning to see how important it is for us to rescue those trapped in the cesspool of the **Well-Oiled Machine** as they are being "*led to the slaughter*"?[29]

Oh yeah. Read on.

rescue those who are perishing

"Rescue those who are being taken away to death, and those
who are staggering to slaughter, O hold them back."
Proverbs 24:12

Rescue Those Who Are Perishing

The Scriptural battle cry of the pro-life movement.
A call to spiritual arms— the infamous wake-up call.
The Biblical equivalent of Paul Revere's early warning to a sleeping, infant nation, "The British are coming! The British are coming!"

"Excuse me, but what in the world are you talking about now?"
Once again, glad you asked.

You see, I've been doing some serious thinking lately— some *soul-searching* kind of thinking. The kind of personal reflection that often leads to a mid-life crisis or a total re-evaluation of everything once held as true and immutable.
Yep, that's me. That's the world I've been living in lately.

So, do you want to know what I've discovered? Do you want to know what fuels my passion? Want to take a quick peek in my underwear drawer...uh, so to speak?
Ok. But first things first.

The CPC of Sevier County

In the early 1990's the pro-life movement was the flavor of the month within Christian circles. Everybody was talking about it. Everybody had an opinion about it. Yet only a few, or so it seemed, were actually *involved* in the fray.

Some of the marquee players were as different as night and day, as different as Laverne and Shirley. You had the iconic, larger-than-life heroes like James Dobson and *Focus on the Family* riding tall in the saddle, uncompromising, tirelessly fighting for the life of the unborn, much like a modern day John Wayne, Glenn Ford or Joan of Arc. On the flip side of the coin you had the likes of a rogue Randall Terry and *Operation Rescue* with their prayer vigils, body blockades and doctrine of Civil Disobedience. For those of us involved up to our armpits in the fight for the life of the unborn, these two men represented the *best* Christianity had to offer at that crucial time in the life of the church. They were living examples of the teachings of Christ.

It was also the era of *Life Chains*— an unprecedented time of unity when entire communities would put aside their petty differences and stand together, side by side, church by church, denomination by denomination— boldly holding signs that testified to all that *Abortion Kills Children* and *Jesus Heals and Forgives*.

Do you remember those days? Boy, I sure do.

It was a time of true, "hands-to-the-plow" type of ministry.[1] A time when it felt *good* to be a Christian and a time when we really believed we could make a difference in our world and community.

Pastors and churches soon discovered they could no longer hide in the shadows, in the safe, grey areas between apathy and action. The church was forced to choose, to take a stand on what society defined as a *political* issue. They had to stop riding the fence, step up to the challenge, and be counted. Why? Because somehow the church had to contend with a swelling, grassroots army of zealots that expected... no, that *demanded* more from their leaders than a simple Sunday sermon and lame Bumper Sticker theology.

No time to sit on the fence. No time for mere words. You either got your hands dirty doing God's work or you just sat on your bum and talked about it.

It was a time of Christian activism.

But more importantly, it was a wondrous time of personal accountability and responsibility.

Some preachers would stand behind their pulpits and rail against the evils of Christian activism and defiantly proclaim whether they were '*fer* or '*agin* what others were doing in the name of Christ for the helpless unborn. Then their congregations, like flocks of migrating geese, would dutifully file out of the church and into the closest Denny's for the $4.99 Grand Slam Special to discuss whether they were '*fer* or '*agin* what the preacher said he was '*fer* or '*agin*. Ah, the same typical kind of church junk we've got today. Critically picking the fruit of another's tree and judging it against your own barren branches.

"Well, that may be so. But *if* I were to get involved in the Pro-Life Movement, I would do it this way or that way and *not* like *they* are doing it…"

In other words, my *if* would be better than their *doing*— *if* I decide to get involved, which, of course, I won't. Classic armchair quarterback stuff. Never seems to change.

And all the while— little babies died.

Kind of makes it easy to understand how Jesus could vomit the church out of His mouth, doesn't it?[2]

It's also easy to understand how Christian zealots almost always end up as members of the **Love Jesus, Hate Church** fraternity.

Anyway, back to the time that was.

It was a time long before the great watering-down epidemic that infected the church in the late 1990s and continues unchecked today. It was long before Promise Keepers captured our attention with its addictive shock and awe stadium experience and parade of popular and wannabe popular Christian leaders. Long before the *seeker* and their wants became the *goal* and focus of our worship. And long before the slew of New York Times bestselling books that would treat God as someone waiting to serve us and not as the Supreme Creator of the Universe.

You know those books, don't you? You may even have a couple of them on your shelves at home.

First, there was the **Prayer of Jabez** with its primary focus on the "Oh, that You would bless *me* indeed, and enlarge *my* territory"— with the emphasis always on the feel-good *me* aspect of the Christian life.

So popular was the idea that God wanted to bless us and enlarge our territory that it spawned a steady line of other money-making clones.

The Prayer of Jabez for Women

The Prayer of Jabez for Kids and then for Teens

The Prayer of Jabez for Little Ones

The Prayer of Jabez Devotional
The Prayer of Jabez Music – The Worship Experience
The Prayer of Jabez Day to Day Calendar
The Prayer of Jabez Special Edition
The Prayer of Jabez Journal
The Prayer of Jabez Bible Study
The Prayer of Jabez… ah, enough!

Soon there'll be the Son of Jabez or the Bride of Jabez or maybe Return to the Planet of Jabez or something like that.

I think you get the point.

Then, in rapid succession, there was the **Purpose Driven Life** craze and the franchised **40 Days of Purpose** that has quickly become the standard of acceptance within the Pastor Conference circuits, something akin to a secret handshake or a special decoder ring ordered from the back of an Ovaltine box.[3]

Finally, there's Joel Osteen's **Your Best Life Now** bestseller that tells us how to have favor with those around us in order to get God to do our bidding. For example, if you find yourself in a crowded restaurant and you're in a hurry, Osteen suggests saying the following prayer (or incantation) to get God to move on your behalf: "Father, I thank You that I have favor with this hostess and she's going to seat me soon."

Ugh. That's exactly why Jesus died, isn't it? You know, to make sure the hostess seats my party before someone else who has been waiting longer!

But that's a subject for another time and another chapter.

And who knows what feel-good, man-exalting, future bestselling book is just around the corner waiting to be devoured by hungry Believers wishing, as Paul said, to have their "ears tickled."[4]

Love Means Never Having to Say You're Sorry

In the early fall of 1990 my wife and I were led by the Lord to begin the Crisis Pregnancy Center of Sevier County in an old church building we were able to rent. My family and I lived in the Sunday school rooms and converted the sanctuary into offices, a counseling center and dormitory-style housing for the unwed mothers that came to live with us because of their decision to Choose Life.

Oh yes, sometimes doing right, by Choosing Life, actually leads to homelessness.

It was one of the greatest times in my spiritual life! We experienced, day by day, God's miracles and the joy of one-on-one times of life-changing ministry. No fluff, just ministry.

During that time, the one verse of Scripture that captured the focus of what we did and described our motivation of sorts came from the 24th chapter of the book of Proverbs.

It reads:

> Deliver those who are being taken away to death,
> and those who are staggering to slaughter,
> Oh hold them back.[5]

For us, this was our battle cry and our marching orders. It was the very words of the Lord commanding Karen and me— and all Christians for that matter— to stand for and protect those who couldn't fend for themselves. It was our ministry to deliver those who were literally being led to their slaughter. And in the late 80's and early 90's, no group of people in our country fit that description more than the helpless unborn.

Hence, the ministry of the Crisis Pregnancy Center of Sevier County was born.

By now you're probably wondering what all of this has to do with the title of this book. I mean, how does the pro-life movement relate to those who **Love Jesus** and **Hate Church**? Where's the connection? What's the point?

Belly Up to the Bar

Think about it.

For most of us, the idea of church often conjures up the image of stately red brick buildings with tall, white, majestic steeples that point like an arrow straight into the heart of God. For others, church gives us the warm, cozy feelings of nostalgia, the pleasant memories of good-times long past. We fondly think of Sunday school with its Picture Bibles, flannel graphs, warm cherry Kool-Aid, and hard oatmeal cookies. We remember Christmas plays and living nativities and shepherds' costumes made from mom's best bath towels and dad's favorite pale-blue robe. There was VBS and sword drills and Tootsie Rolls and Labor Day picnics and… well, the list can go on and on.

Church was portrayed as a place of safety and security, a living sanctuary where Christians could take shelter from the oppressive hurt and abuse the world tends to dish out on its inhabitants. It was a place of worship, a place of love, of acceptance, and mutual ministry.

The Church was the *one* place on earth where you never feared being hurt or mistreated or misunderstood or belittled or needlessly offended or persecuted or slandered or wronged or berated. Why?

"Because church is just like one big ol' happy family. Right?"

Well, not always. Not really.

Every Sunday, hidden among masses of people that dutifully file in and out of church services across the land, there is an ever-growing army of disgruntled and disillusioned Believers that carry with them the battle scars they receive on the frontlines of Church. This group of walking wounded, their Purple Heart in hand, are interwoven into the very membership fabric of our congregations. They're disguised, cloaked, concealed behind a well-dressed façade that smiles and says, "How are you today? Just fine. And you?" and then moves on. They're detached. Wary. Reluctant to allow the pain they've experienced in Church to be inflicted upon them, and their families, again.

"Don't come any closer. Stay back. I don't want to be hurt again."

And this group just keeps getting larger.

Church splits, moral failures, deacon's meetings, gossip, financial budgets, "the pastor didn't call me when I was sick", arguments, hymns versus choruses, young versus old, family church dynasty versus the "new kids on the church block", building programs, tithing, pride, the annual Church Business Meetings, "look, those people sat in my seat", and King James going one-on-one with everybody else... ah, you name it. They all take their toll.

It's like a young man or woman who has lost their virginity and is desperately trying to right the wrong, trying to turn back the clock in a futile attempt to make things like they were once before.

Well, you can't. You can *never* go back to the way it was before.

Once the bottle is broken and the innocence is spilled, you can *never* put it back into the bottle again. You *never* move from **Love Jesus, Hate Church** to Love Jesus, Love Church. There's no round-trip ticket. No return fare. It's simply a one-way ride from intimacy to disengagement, from reckless abandon to cautious reserve, from child-like delight to disillusionment and despair— or, in other words, from love to hate.

And every day it seems the ranks of the **Love Jesus, Hate Church** army swells.

As a pastor and a minister for the past 20 years, I have seen and experienced firsthand the spiritual trauma and emotional havoc that **Love Jesus, Hate Church** situations can wreak on the hearts and minds of those who attend church— on those staggering to the slaughter. I've seen countless people bounce into church with exuberance, contagious excitement, literally wide-eyed with awe and expectation of what the Lord was going to do in their lives and in the life of their church. And sadly, like spooked cattle, I've also seen these same people leave the church in droves, vowing never to return. Those same wide eyes now vacant and blackened by a church fight and the inevitable loss of their child-like innocence— the painful loss of their spiritual virginity. I have heard their cries and have seen their tears— and I've seen this cycle repeated year after year after year.

The pain and hurt from one of countless **Love Jesus, Hate Church** encounters is not just limited to the injured parties. No, the hurt goes much deeper and the ripple effects much wider. Many, unfortunately, will pass their burdens down to their own children, creating something like a generational curse that keeps growing with no end in sight. And this curse, like a systemic **Love Jesus, Hate Church** virus, infects and aggressively attacks the very roots of the Believer's view of the Christian community. It destroys the Believer's sense of acceptance and mutual respect. It turns a loving, trusting church family into a team of spoiled, self-seeking free agents.

And it most certainly grieves the Lord.

A New Evil For a New Day

So what are we to do?

Let me close this chapter by telling you that I still exist under the same divine mandate as I did back then. Although I'm no longer the Director of the CPC in Sevier County, I still hold dear the Lord's command to "rescue and deliver those being led away to the slaughter." I still stand for those who are "staggering unto destruction."

Same ministry. Different focus.

Today there's a *new* evil in the land that threatens to snuff out the life of the innocent— of those being led away to slaughter. And this evil is far more insidious, far more heinous than any abortion clinic or pro-choice Nazi that demands the blood of the unborn to satisfy their lust for happiness.

No, I'm not talking about the influx of homosexuality in our culture or the rapid, saturating spread of drugs or sex.

Sorry, it's nothing quite so simple or so evident.

The greatest *evil* in our society today, the greatest instrument of potential hurt and destruction we as Believers face is what I have just described above: **The Church**!

Yes. It's the institution that you and I are probably members of right now!

Remember, we're not talking about the church that Christ died for, the *called-out ones*— but the church of our own making. Our own Frankenstein. The church Christ wants to vomit out of His mouth.[6]

The Well-Oiled Machine.

You want a ministry?

Ok, how 'bout spending the rest of your life delivering people from the slaughter that takes place behind the walls of church.

Stand firm for truth, no matter how much it might cost you.

For Christ's sake, be different! And then ask the Lord to use you to *make* a difference.

Come and join us. Become a **Love Jesus**, **Hate Church** zealot and help us, one life at a time, depopulate the ranks of those who **Love Jesus** and **Hate Church** by "rescuing those being led away to slaughter."

"How?" you wonder.

First, by making sure you're a true, sold-out, Biblical Christian yourself.

And *then*…well,— we will be discussing more about *"then"* in the next section.

part two

HOLINESS, CHILD-LIKE FAITH AND OTHER STUFF WE REALLY DON'T WANT TO TALK ABOUT

HOW TO GET OUT OF THE NASTY MESS WE HAVE CREATED

two truths, two paths— one choice

"When I'm on stage, I'm trying to do one thing: bring
people joy. Just like church does. People don't go to church
to find trouble, they go there to lose it."
James Brown (1920-)

Got a Question for You

Question: What's the staying power of the church, the *called-out ones*? What's the bond, the triple-tough alloy that welds the *called-out ones* together? What gives the church its spiritual power to stand against the darkness and the supreme confidence to know that the very gates of Hell will not prevail against her?[1]

What is it?

Answer: It's none other than the abiding presence of the Holy Spirit. The incomprehensible and indescribable promise of Jesus that was phenomenally fulfilled in Acts 2. Remember?

Good. Then let's take a look back into the pages of Scripture together, shall we?

How Important is the Holy Spirit?

"Are you serious?"

Like duh! Of course, I'm serious.

How important is the Holy Spirit?

Prophet, Priest and King

In the Old Testament, the one primary attribute and non-negotiable characteristic required to turn an ordinary, everyday, "just flesh and bone" man into a spiritual prophet of God was the presence of the Holy Spirit. Over and over again we see phrases in the Old Testament such as, "And the Spirit of God came upon them and they began to prophesy." The Holy Spirit would come upon those He chose and supernaturally turn them into spokesmen for God. Prophets— the heroes of old. They were like heavenly Press Agents giving Confidential Briefings directly from the throne room of God.

God didn't play favorites. He wasn't *then*, nor is He *now*, a respecter of persons.[2] It didn't matter to Him what their last name was or where they graduated from college. He didn't care if they were blue collar, white collar, or no collar at all. He wasn't even interested in whether they wore boxers or briefs.

No, it was *only* when the Holy Spirit came upon a man of God's choosing that he was able to climb the corporate ladder and be promoted to the level of prophet. Or, maybe more like, *elevated* to that office.

Bottom line: No Holy Spirit. No prophet of God. Nuthin'!

It's also important to remember that in the Old Testament, the Holy Spirit didn't reside or abide with people the way He does today. Why? Because all of the Old Testament saints shared a genetic, defective, pre-Acts 2 blood type.

Think about it.

If you were one of the wandering travelers that left Egypt with Moses and wanted to be where the Lord was, *you* had to make the journey and travel to Mount Zion. God didn't come to you. It was *your* responsibility to find out exactly where the Lord was and then align your life to His. You're the one who had to put in the miles. You had to burn your own gas.

It was basically *your* responsibility.

Moses would smile, wave to his family and then disappear into the tabernacle for his face-to-face meeting with God. And, as the Scriptures tell us, when Moses would finally emerge from the tabernacle, his face would be glowing— like a lingering residue, resonating from the Glory of God.[3]

The people would come up to Moses and ask him, implore him, to tell them what God had said. What's the plan? The next move?

In other words, "Hey Mo. You just spoke with God. What'd He havta say? What's going on? What's He got up His sleeve?"

"What's the buzz, tell me what's happening."[4]

If for some reason you weren't numbered among the throng of cameras, microphones, and reporters jockeying for position at the mouth of the tabernacle— you were flat out of luck. You missed Moses giving his Confidential Briefing. There were no questions and answers. No sound bites for the eleven o'clock news. No press releases. Nothing. If you chose, for example, to remain secluded in your tent munching on Cheese Nips and watching reruns of *Everybody Loves Raymond*, you missed out on the Presence of God. You were left out in the dark. Clueless.

To be in the *know*, you had to be around the action.

Now, It's A Whole New Ball Game

In the New Testament all that changed.

Once we venture past the red ink in our Bibles, we find we're now transformed, morphed if you will, from a group of half-hearted seekers into a kingdom of priests.[5] Whether we feel like priests or not, that's exactly what Scripture now calls us. We're also identified as a royal priesthood.[6] There's no longer the long, arduous trek to God or the anxious wait for Him to appear and grant us an audience like the elusive Wizard of Oz. You'll never hear the words, as Dorothy did from the lips of the incredulous gatekeeper to the Emerald City— "You want to see the Wizard? Why no one has ever seen the Wizard. I've never even seen the Wizard. Go away. Come back tomorrow."[7]

None of that will ever happen to you, or to me— or to any child of God. A long, laborious, exhausting pilgrimage to God is no longer necessary. It's a thing of the past. Banished. Why? Because the Holy Spirit now resides in us! He's already here! He actually takes up residence in our beings. Which, if you think about it, makes us individual tabernacles, a sanctuary of the Living God. We are the dwelling place of the Almighty.

"Heavy stuff," as Link from the Mod Squad would say.

It lights my fire when I dwell on that blessing! How about you?

At the birth of the church, when the promised event happened in Acts 2 and the Holy Spirit came and filled each Believer with the very Presence of God, they literally became the individual mouthpieces of God. They would speak His Word as the Spirit compelled them— as the Spirit gave them utterance.[8] Why? Because they now belonged to, and were empowered by, the Lord.

We also know, by virtue of the incredible gift we've been given since Acts 2, that we don't have to make an appointment to speak with a prophet in order to hear from God. We don't need God to speak to us through someone else. Why? Because God speaks to each one of us through His Spirit.

We don't have to go to a priest to beg him to make atonement for our sins. Or, at the very least, have him tell us what *we* must do to make God love us again or become acceptable in His presence.

No thanks.

No penance wanted and no penance needed.

We don't have to systematically offer various kinds of sacrifices to somehow appease our God.

We don't have to walk around on cut glass, barefoot, or frantically recite all sorts of mindless mantras for God to receive us again as His children.

We don't even have to ask someone in a robe to pray for us. Or even faithfully attend church, for that matter. Why? Because we already have a direct line— a dedicated, broadband, high-speed connection, to Jesus Christ. We can pray anytime we want with the assurance that He hears us.[9] We can talk *to* and hear *from* God ourselves— without any middleman. We can buy wholesale, directly from God's factory.

It's better than having a Sam's Club Card in heaven.

As Christians, you and I are destined to become "little Christs" and little ambassadors, for Him.[10]

It's our heritage.

The very reason we were created.

News Bulletin from the Throne

And suddenly, like a bolt of lightening, it dawned on me that you and I already possess the *one* central, undeniable quality that made Daniel and Ezekiel and Isaiah the men that they were. We already possess what made them prophets of God and heroes of the faith. The realization hit me hard, broadside, like a linebacker for the Bears, that there's no inherent difference between the heroes of the Old Testament— those great men of old we admire and hold up as the standard of faith— and the potential heroes of our day.[11] Uh, that's you and me, by the way. There's no inherent difference between them and us. None at all. God spoke to them and let His Spirit reside within them— for a season. And God has spoken to us and has allowed His Spirit to baptize and abide with us— and remain.

Incredible!
To remain.
Forever!

He has already equipped you as much as He equipped Ezekiel or Daniel or the rest of those we rightly place on such high spiritual pedestals.

Therefore, the same principles that applied to the prophetic life of those in the Old Testament also apply to us today.

Careful Now, Preacher. Don't Get Carried Away!

Pastors, for the most part, don't particularly relish the idea of preaching the kind of stuff I'm sharing with you now because it tends to give their congregation too much power and authority. And that always makes for a tough time at the Monthly Business Meeting. Often shortens their tenure at the church.

Pastors also have this fear that a *self*-proclaimed prophet might stand up in the middle of one of his sermons and spew off some prophetic utterances, allegedly from God, about how this cute young tart sitting on the third row should be more modest and wear longer dresses in public or how God wants the church to purchase softball uniforms for the Men's Brotherhood League from his brother-in-law's struggling screen printing business. Or maybe… well, I think you get the point.

But the simple reality is this: If you're a Believer in Jesus Christ, the Holy Spirit resides in you. Permanently. The Bible says that He is your deposit, your guarantee of your future inheritance to come.[12]

No Holy Spirit— and you ain't going to heaven.

No Holy Spirit— and you're not called by His name.

No Holy Spirit— and you're not saved. Case closed, end of argument. Fineto!

But if the Holy Spirit, God Himself, resides in you, then He wants to shine His goodness through you to others for the whole world to see. In fact, that's exactly what Jesus was talking about when He spoke about not placing a lamp under a bucket but putting it on the table for the entire world to see.[13]

In other words, what the Lord did for the prophets of old is exactly what He wants to do for each of us— for His church, His *called-out ones*, today.

"Ok, I'm with you so far. What does God want to do through me?"
Good question. Actually, it's a *great* question!
Let's take a look at the answer together.

This Thing Called *Church*

In Luke 24, we see Jesus carefully instructing His disciples and telling them not to do anything until they received the power He promised them back in John 14.[14]

"Don't do anything," He was saying. "Nothing. Zero. Zilch."

They were to stay in Jerusalem until they were supernaturally clothed with power from on high. "You are My witnesses of these things," Jesus told them, "and behold, I am sending forth the promise of My Father. You are to stay in the city until you are clothed with power from on high."[15]

We all know what happened in Jerusalem, just ten days later at the celebration of the Feast of Pentecost, when the church was born and the promise of the Father was mightily fulfilled. The Scriptures record for us in specific, meticulous detail the events of Acts 2 when the Holy Spirit came to abide with the 120 in the upper room and the promise of Jesus was consummated in a parade of awesome, explosive power.[16] These ordinary men were now filled with the extraordinary Promise and did some incredible, some truly *unbelievable* things in the power of the Holy Spirit!

Some *unparalleled* things, from that time until today!

These uneducated, often erratic, unpredictably weak, double-minded fishermen and common day laborers now stood boldly against a hostile crowd and passionately preached a sermon that revealed a doctorate level understanding of the Old Testament. Read it for yourself in Acts 2:14-36.

I mean, who are these guys?

Where did they get their knowledge and understanding of the Scriptures?

Where did their courage come from?

What's going on here?

If this event happened in *our* time and in *our* present church culture, we would probably dismiss the miracle as a clever slight-of-hand deception and digress into a deeply heated discussion about important issues such as, "How much is this gonna cost?" Or, "I don't care what you think, I have my own opinion." Maybe, "Hey, I don't want to do it that way, I have my own ideas." Or finally, the big clincher, the granddaddy of them all… "But, we've never done it *that* way before!"

Whew. Sound familiar?

Instead, what these guys did in Acts 2:42 and throughout the rest of the chapter literally staggers the mind— especially the ever-popular 21st Century, "I've-got-it-all-together and don't need nothing" religious mindset in America. These young Believers actually had the nerve, the arrogant audacity, to flesh out what they believed. They were actually convinced that the teachings of Jesus were to be obeyed and not just batted around and debated like one of the many prevailing philosophies or lofty ideals of the day.

They actually believed, and I mean *really* believed, that the Christian life they had embraced with their whole being was truly for "living" and not just for "preaching" and was unquestionably light-years ahead of anything this world had to offer. The early *called-out ones* literally acted and functioned, day by day, like Jesus was their Lord and the Spirit of God made His abode in them.

Imagine that!

They wore their faith on their sleeve, out in the open, like a badge of honor— for the entire world to see.

Today, I guess that would make them that...well, that "**F**" word.

Remember?

Oh yeah. It would make them *fanatics*.

And I'm a fan of the fanatics. Read on.

i'm a fan of the fanatics

"A fanatic is someone who loves Jesus more than you."
Steve McCranie, *Love Jesus, Hate Church*

A Fan of the Fanatics

The early *called-out ones* were able to put aside the one trapping, the one hidden, life-threatening cancer that seems to keep us confined to life-support and stuck in apathy like superglue. Unlike the *called-out ones* of today, they were somehow able to miraculously grasp and understand the key truth of Jesus' teaching that our lives no longer belong to ourselves— we have died and now live in Him.[1] The truth that clearly states we have been bought with a price and are no longer our own.[2] They lived in the blessed realm that Jesus was the Lord of everything they possessed and, therefore, they were to treat each other better than closest kin, better than family.

They were to consider each other more important than they considered themselves.[3]

To me, *that* seems like the greatest of all the Acts 2 miracles. Utterly amazing.

Look what happened.

If *anyone* had a need, regardless of where they worked, went to school, family size, racial or ethnic background— regardless of who they voted for in the last election, how they dressed, or what kind of music they listened to, regardless of who they rooted for during the Super Bowl or on what side of the fence they fell on such controversial issues as defense spending, women's rights, or the separation of church and state— if *anyone* had a need, the early *called-out ones* felt compelled to meet that need based solely on the merits of the gift Christ had freely bestowed on them.

And what gift was that? The gift of His Spirit.

Where did the early church get the resources to meet the needs of others? Did they come from the Church Budget or the Benevolence Fund? Did they take up a "love offering" at the end of a mid-week service? Did they hit-up the Salvation Army or the local Homeless Shelter for help?

Nope.

Everything that was given, everything the church released and placed into the needy hands of someone else came personally from the pockets and checkbooks of the other Spirit-filled *called-out ones* who had unselfishly jettisoned their personal possessions for the benefit of others. Wow! They physically removed a spiritual stumbling block that often tends to anchor us to this world's mindset and values.[4] As it states, "and *all* those who had believed were together and had *all things in common*; and they began selling their property and possessions and were sharing them with *all*, as *anyone* might have need."[5]

Shhh. Quiet now. Listen closely. I think I can hear the sound of the church of today voicing its dismay over this radical way of thinking. Can you hear them? The long, rambling, single train of horrified panic as they come to grips with what the first church was all about.

"We can't do *that* because people will take advantage of us and we'll end up being nothing and having nothing when we retire and all our stuff will belong to somebody else and we worked hard for all that stuff and it's not fair and if we give all our stuff to others then we'll be the needy ones and then we'll have to ask others for help and I don't want to do that because it will make others feel about me the same way I feel about them and I won't be successful and..."

Yawn.

In our culture we categorically reject the early *called-out ones'* way of living out their faith in Christ because it violates one of the core, inalienable virtues we esteem above all others. You know, the virtue of self-determination, of self-actualization. The right we claim to call our *own* shots, to chart our *own* course, and be the master of our *own* destiny. The, "Look bub, I made it my *own* way. I picked myself up by my *own* bootstraps. I'm a self-made man. Therefore, I don't have a problem giving to others who are in need; I just don't ever want anyone to have to give to me, to meet my needs. I can take care of myself."

Or, my vote counts.

I'm important.

I have an opinion.

"I coulda been a contender."[6]

Uh, I think the Bible calls that pride.

The early *called-out ones* weren't like that because they realized that Christ, as the Sovereign Lord, was really the head of everything.

What Have You Learned, Dorothy?

So the church, however you want to define it, actually has two options.

We can either let Christ be the head of our congregations by asking and inviting Him to be the Sovereign Lord in each of our individual lives, or we can determine to call all the shots in His Kingdom ourselves. By proxy, like spoiled, stubborn, rebellious children. It can really be no other way.

There is, unfortunately, no third option.

No escape pod.

And no silver parachute.

He is either Lord over each of us or we, by default, will act and function as lord over His church. I don't know about you, but it has been my experience in the corporate church setting that it's the people, the membership of the congregation, who exclusively call the shots.[7] It's *never* the Lord. And, if you were brutally honest with yourself, you'd have to admit that's true.

Painful, yes. But true, nonetheless.

Think back and review your own personal experience with the church. You've heard it all before, "I have *my* vote, I have *my* opinion, and I have *my* rights. I like this and I don't like that. Did I give you permission to go there, use that or try something new?" versus letting Christ be the head of everything.

Let's take a brief, summary overview of some Scriptures that deal with this living organism known as the church and the natural, inevitable outcome of choosing either option presented to us.

First, Paul's letter to the church at Ephesus: "And He put all things in subjection under His (Jesus) feet, and gave Him (Jesus) as head over all things to the church, which is His (Jesus) body, the fullness of Him (Jesus) who fills all in all."[8]

Now, if Jesus is the Sovereign Lord of my life and He is also the Sovereign Lord of your life, then when the two of us come together as a church, the *called-out ones*, who would be the Sovereign Lord of this church entity? Exactly! The same Person who is the Sovereign Lord of our individual lives will also be the Sovereign Lord when those individuals come together in mass as a group.

Just think:

"The sum total of the composite natures of the individual parts of the Body will determine the nature of the whole Body."

Doesn't that seem logical to you?

Or, "The sum of the square roots of any two sides of an isosceles triangle is equal to the square root of the remaining side. Oh joy! Rapture! I've got a brain!" said the Scarecrow to the Wizard of Oz.

Uh, let me describe it another way.

Suppose a local church gathering is made up of only three individual Believers— say Frank, Tom and Brad. Now suppose that Christ is the Sovereign Lord, without reservation, in Frank's life but Tom and Brad aren't exactly sure if they want to relinquish their control to the Lord in this matter. After all, they're used to calling their own shots and making their own decisions based pretty much on what they feel is right, just, or expedient.

"God gave us a mind," they would say, chest out and thumbs hooked in their suspenders, "and He expects us to use it."

When the three of them come together to worship, or to *do* church, or to make decisions for the Body of Christ— two-thirds of this body is basically ruled and governed by whom?

Yep. That's right. Self.

And only one-third is ruled by Christ.

What happens then? Factions, gossip, anger, backbiting, divisions and all the other things that we're warned about in Scripture.[9]

Second Verse, Same as the First

Once again, we have only two options.

We can allow Christ to assume the rightful position that belongs solely to Him as the Lord of our lives and, by definition, the Lord of our *called-out ones* when other like-minded Believers who share the same passion are present. Remember, when those who *also* have Christ at the center of their being as their Sovereign Lord come together for corporate worship, or ministry, or service, or prayer— that specific Body of Believers is made up in like fashion. It has the same nature, the same Spirit. Why? It has Christ as the head of His Body because Christ is also the head of the individual members that make up His Body.

Or, like the Burger King slogan, if we say, "Have It Your Way", then we end up with what the following Scriptures warn about. You can look them up for yourselves if you want. But it's pretty depressing.

Let's take a quick preview of **Church: Man's Way**.

Paul, in I Corinthians 1:11-12 talks about **quarrels** between people, members of Christ's Body, His beloved church. Ouch![10]

Pride and **strife** are rebuked in I Corinthians 3: 1-7.[11] Paul is saying, "Some of you guys say you're from this camp and follow this religious teacher. Then some of you say you're in this other camp with this other guy. And some of you like this and some of you like that…and some of you think this is correct and some of you don't and…gee, why are you doing all this? Who has led you astray? Within the church, the *called-out ones*, it's *never* about my opinions or your opinions or what I want or what you want. It's always about Christ and Him alone. Get it? Christ and Christ alone!"

In I Corinthians 6:1-11, Paul talks about the misuse of our supposed personal rights by **defrauding** one another.[12] He talks about the fact that some of the church, the *called-out ones*, are so carnal-minded and 21st Century indoctrinated in their thinking that they're hiring attorneys, demanding restitution, and suing each other in court. "How is God honored in all that?" Paul asks. "Can't two Christians come together and agree on something under the auspices of the Lord Jesus Christ rather than going to some secular judge to have him sort it out? Why demand your rights? Why not rather be wronged? Why not rather be defrauded? On the contrary, you yourselves wrong and defraud each other and you do this even to your brethren."[13]

Not to make light of it, but I can hear Gomer Pyle straining his voice in chastisement of the church, saying, "Shame, shame, shame."

Want more?

How about **gossip, slander, strife, jealously, impurity, immorality** and **sensuality** we see in 2 Corinthians 12:20-21.[14] Sounds like several of the churches I've pastored in the past.

Think about it.

Proverbs tells us that "He who goes about as a slanderer reveals secrets. Therefore do not associate with a gossip."[15] Wow. And often we allow the guilty parties to serve in leadership capacities within our churches today and do nothing about their gossip.

"After all, they're friends." Yeah, some friends.

The Hatfields and McCoys

But for me, the most pitiful and pathetic picture of the results of a man-governed church, the one which I believe grieves the Spirit of God the most, is found in Philippians 4:2-3.[16] Here Paul is fervently urging these two, Eudoia and Syntyche, to try to **live in harmony** with one another. Why? Because their quarrel, whatever it was about, was causing division among Christ's Body and was separating good friends.

I can hear the report to Paul now.

"Paul, you know those two, they're always bickering at church. Never a kind word to say to each other. And now each of their families are taking sides and our whole congregation is on the verge of a split. Man, I wish those two would just bury the hatchet (and not in each other's back) and let's get on with serving our Lord."

Paul's response went something like this, "I urge Eudonia and Syntyche (or any name you want to place there from your own church experience) to live in harmony in the Lord. Come on, put whatever it is that has upset you aside. Life is too short. Indeed, true companions, I ask you also to help these two resolve this. Would somebody help these two who are arguing all the time? These are two friends who at one time shared in the struggles of the call of the gospel together with Clement and also the rest of my fellow workers whose names are in the book of life. For God's sake would somebody mature step up to the plate and please get these two together and resolve this matter and teach these two to live in harmony with each other and stop this constant, irritating pettiness and bickering in the church! Man, give me a break! Like I don't have enough to deal with already without having to settle your immature squabbles."

In other words, would you, the church, the *called-out ones*, show yourself mature and make disciples of these two before this turns into a first-class spitting contest and not only destroys the testimony and integrity of the church, but also defames the very Name of Christ?

Would *somebody*, for Christ's sake, do *something*?

Now, 2,000 Years Later...

Sadly, for 2,000 years all of Christendom has read about this petty and childlike argument among those two in the church at Philippi. For almost two millennia we have read the account and wondered what it was that was so important that Paul had to address it in his letter to the church.

Was it some doctrinal deviation that had slithered into the church under the radar of the elders and threatened to lead the flock astray into heresy?

Did it have something to do with the mission of the church, the holiness of God, or the testimony of our Lord Jesus?

Probably not.

If it was like most church squabbles, it undoubtedly had to do with someone sitting in someone else's chair, or who was going to sing the lead solo in the Easter Cantata or maybe the simple fact... no, the *unforgivable* sin, that the "preacher didn't shake my hand" when I left the Sunday service.

"Scarred me for life! I'm never coming back!"

Yep, it was probably something like we fight about today in our man-governed, self-centered, Spirit-starved church. Right?

You know, someday we're going to bump into those two in heaven. Mark my words, when we do I'm going to make it a point to ask them what was so important and so vital to the very survival of the church that it caused such a deep division at that time. Can you imagine what they will say?

"So, what were you two fighting about anyway?"

"You know, I don't even remember what it was about now. I mean, it seemed so important at the time. I forgot about a 1,000 years ago."

How embarrassingly petty and pathetic it is for us when Christ doesn't become the head and Sovereign Lord of our lives.

What position have you given the Lord in your life?

What's Next?

How are you feeling about now? Flustered? Irritated? Maybe a bit mad?

Good. Emotion right now is a good thing. It shows you still care. That you're still alive.

For me, all of this talk about where the church is today and where it should be leaves a bitter taste in my mouth. It kind of makes me sick to my stomach.

And, know what? I'm not alone. I'm in some good company.

Read on.

projectile vomit— and the sunday morning worship service

"The Church says that the Earth is flat, but I know that it is
round. For I have seen the shadow on the moon and I have
more faith in the shadow than in the Church."
Ferdinand Magellan (1480-1521)

For a number of years I've really anguished over all of this stuff
we've been talking about. I agonized over the apparent apathy, the blatant
hypocrisy, and the absolute absence of any semblance of a positive testimony
of the church in my generation. I mean, it literally tore me up and ate away
at my insides. Made me angry. Mad.

Time and time again I would find myself asking the Lord, "Why do I
find church so nauseating? Why do I let all of it get under my skin? Tell me,
why does it bother me so much, Lord? Is there something I'm missing? Is
there something good and honorable and Christ-like about church that maybe
I'm just not seeing? Am I blind? Is there something wrong with me? Lord,
why do I **Love Jesus** and **Hate Church**?"

Make no mistake, I really **do** find what we flippantly pass off as *church*
today incredibly, indescribably, and excruciatingly nauseating. It's sickening
to the core. I get physically ill when I think about all the countless committee
meetings I've had to attend over the last 20 years or so that accomplished
nothing and amounted to little more than a huge waste of time. I'm disgusted

by the unending cycle of gossip I've heard over the years from the lips of supposed friends, and the continued bickering and backbiting between families or groups of families within the church. It's gut wrenching, beyond description, to see the torrent of carnality we try to pawn off as *Christianity* today. I mean, it literally makes me sick to my stomach.

Think for a moment.

You've got one group of self-righteous saints smugly seated in the pews to the left who haven't said a kind word to this other group seated in the pews to the right because of some hard feelings or hurtful words that were spoken between them long before Nixon resigned from office. It's really sad.

I should know. I've got the scars to show.

From the pastor's perspective it gets even worse.

The poor pastor has to stand behind the pulpit as God's spokesman each Sunday and try to preach and proclaim the Word of God to the people entrusted to his care. And what does he see more often than not? He looks out to see half the congregation with a scowl etched on their faces, arms folded in defiance, eyes steeled, both hearts and minds closed tight, because something didn't go their way or a member of their group (or family, click, gang, posse, lynch-mob or whatever…) got their feelings hurt. Oh, poor little Boo-Boo Kitty.

Mandatory Announcement: The church service must start at exactly 11:00 am and be punctually concluded no later than 12:00, noon, regardless of what the Lord may be doing in His service. No deviations allowed. No exceptions. Why?

"Hey, I don't want to have to wait in line at the Steak House today, preacher. You need to say what you have to say and be done by noon. We've all got other things to do today, you know."

Before your Sunday morning worship service, as the bulletins (playbills as they are called in the secular world) are distributed to the congregation, the members of the Finance Committee also hand out the upcoming Budget and Financial Report spreadsheets because, "Everyone has to have a budget to look at, preacher. We're gonna have a vote a week from next Sunday. Don't you remember?"

Then, all during the praise and worship time, and indeed during the sermon, the people there to worship the Lord are, instead, deep in thought as they study the budget, line by line, like they were hired to examine the books of WorldCom or Enron.

"It says here we spent $17.36 last month on long distance phone calls.

Well, I'd like to know who's been using the phone. Who we been callin'? Seems like a big waste of money to me. I'll have to bring that up in the meetin' and find out what's going on."

Do you get the picture?

Need I say more?

It simply got to the point that it was beginning to make me sick. So much so that I dreaded even coming to church— and I was the pastor!

And then something wonderful happened that put everything I was feeling in perspective. The Lord showed me I wasn't alone in what I was feeling. It seems that church today also turns His stomach.

Which means I'm in pretty good company. Real good company.

"So," you may be asking, "that's just *your* experience. What does any of this have to do with us today?"

Ah, everything! Hang on and you'll see.

Living in Laodicea

It's believed by most Biblical scholars that the seven letters to the seven churches, as recorded in chapters two and three of the Revelation, prophetically reveal to us a picture, a snapshot of sorts, of the church age in its entirety from inception to Rapture. This being so, it would naturally follow that we are now living in the Laodicean church age— the seventh, final, and most decadent stage in the history of the church. We are living in the last stage of the church before Christ returns.[1]

The name, "**Laodicea**" literally means "**the rule of the people**" or "**the people rule**." Did you get that? Sound familiar? It's not Christ, but the *people* who rule in this final phase of the history of the church— the Laodicean church phase. It's the membership of the Body of Christ that gives the commands and tells the Head of the Body what to do. Like the proverbial tail wagging the dog. Wow, talk about living in a time when our values and priorities are skewed.

Read carefully, twice if necessary, and see what Jesus had to say about the prevailing character and politically correct mindset of the times in which we now live.

"To the angel of the church in Laodicea write: The Amen, the faithful and true Witness, the Beginning of the creation of God, says this: 'I know your deeds,

117

that you are neither cold nor hot; I wish that you were cold or hot. So because you are lukewarm, and neither hot nor cold, I will spit you out of My mouth. *(Why)* Because you say, "I am rich, and have become wealthy, and have need of nothing," and you do not know that you are wretched and miserable and poor and blind and naked.'"[2]

In other words, Jesus was saying, "You just don't care! You're not passionately for Me and you're not passionately against Me. You just don't seem to give a flip! It's like I'm a non-factor in your life and that turns My stomach. It makes Me sick. All you want to do is come together and go through the motions of your meaningless religious activities in order to make you feel good and then hightail it down the road without so much as a parting thought about how it honors Me or maybe what My desire is for you.

"I wish that you were one way or the other. I wish that you were either hot or cold— for Me or against Me. Love Me or hate Me, but *feel* something! Since you are lukewarm and neither hot nor cold, you make Me sick. You make My stomach churn. You make Me want to vomit you out of My mouth."[3]

Wow. Strong and frightening words.

Did you ever wonder why Jesus feels that way about a lukewarm, non-committed, apathetic church? Or why He feels that way about lukewarm, non-committed, apathetic *called-out ones*? It's basically because of our personal perception about who we are and how important we deem ourselves in our own eyes. We arrogantly claim, "Hey, I'm rich and I've become wealthy. I don't need anything. And I especially don't need You, Lord. I don't need You calling the shots. I don't need You telling me the way I need to live my life. And I especially don't need You to give me a set of rules to follow to be happy. I'm doing fine, just like I am."[4]

In essence, "Get outta my face, will Ya! If I need You I'll call You!"

But from God's perspective, He sees us, the church, the way we really are: "And you do not know that you are wretched, miserable, poor, blind and naked."[5]

My question to each of us who claim to have received Jesus into our lives as our Sovereign Lord is simply this: Do we say, verbally or through our actions and attitudes, like the Laodicean church, "I'm rich, I'm wealthy and I don't need anything? After all, I live in America and maybe I'm a Baptist and maybe I voted Republican in the last election… hey, it really doesn't matter! Fact is, I don't *need* and I certainly don't *want* a Lord in my life. A Savior? Sure. Everybody needs a **Get-Out-Of-Hell-Free** card. But Jesus as my Lord? Absolutely not. I'm pretty much satisfied with how I'm running things in my life right now and I really don't need nuthin' from Him.

"Thanks, but no thanks. I'll pass."

Do you think I'm being a bit too hard? Maybe the ol' shotgun to a knife fight thing again? Nope, don't think so.

Let's be real honest with ourselves, shall we?

When you come to church to worship the Creator of Everything each Sunday, is there any spiritual fruit being produced in your life?[6] When you gather together with your fellow *called-out ones*, do you truly worship the Lord? Look, I'm not talking about singing a few songs or shedding a few emotional tears. I'm not even talking about the dutiful giving of your tithes and offerings or the fact that you've actually *learned* something from the sermon you didn't previously know and have made a commitment to put it into practice from this Sunday on.

No, it's actually much deeper than that.

The Question: Do you really worship? Do you, or have you ever, lost yourself in the ecstatic joy of expressing your adoration to the Lord with all your being? In your gathering of the *called-out ones*, are you lifted beyond where you are and transported into the presence of God?

Do you worship?

If you don't, or if you're not sure— maybe each of us should look again at the very questions about *church* I asked Josh a few chapters ago. Remember?

When you come together for church— do you *worship*?

Do you truly lose yourself in the sheer adoration of the Lord?

Do you offer to Him the unsoiled praises of your lips, the clean hands of faithful service and a heart filled with a love for others?

Or, do you sing some songs that occasionally you like and enjoy and, more often than not, you don't and vainly try to pawn *that* activity off as worship?

After your time of worship each Sunday, have *you* connected with God?

Have *you* been inspired to Godly living?

Have *you* been rebuked or corrected by His Word?

Have *you* been encouraged by the depth and breadth of His Holy Spirit?

Have *you* been exhorted as a Believer to strive for the deeper things of the Spirit?

Have *you* really focused on God and God alone?

Have *you* experienced God's presence in your worship service? If so, great! Wonderful! If not, then why are you even going to your church meetings anyway? I mean, what's the point? Are you hoping to *fake it 'til you make it*? Somehow hoping your faithful attendance will score you some badly needed brownie points with God as an acceptable substitute for spiritual intimacy?

Come on, get real!

Why do you dutifully drag yourself to church every Sunday and Wednesday with the hollow hope that "maybe today God will show up" without ever realizing that you bring His presence with you every time **you** show up?

Again, do you believe the church can change society?

If so, then why is it not happening?

Hey, It'll Get Better, I Just Know It Will!

Actually, no. It won't *ever* get any better than it is today.

Truth is, church life in the lukewarm, apathetic, double-minded, carnal, *the people rule*, Laodicean age will *never* get better. So quit hoping. It just ain't gonna happen. It simply cannot be improved or repackaged.

Do I sound pessimistic? Cynical? I'm really not.

"Just trying to be Biblical, ma'am."

According to Jesus, we live in the Laodicean church age, when the prevailing character trait of those who call themselves Believers is *people rule*. As we have stated before, when the highest virtue within the corporate church setting is the self-centered belief that "I have a voice, a vote— and my vote counts!"— then it's fundamentally impossible for the institution, the vehicle, to improve. Why? Because when the creation rejects the authority of the Creator within the very setting He has established to display His glory— anarchy and self-willed religious rebellion will inevitably take place.

Always has. Always will.

If you're the ruler, the final authority, in your life and Jesus is not much more than a seasoning to flavor your self-willed determination (which, by the way, fits the description of most Christians in America today), then when you come to corporately worship or minister with other *called-out ones* you will, by definition, snatch the authority of the church away from Christ and invest it in yourselves. Why? Because you've already done that in your personal life! Why would you assume that, "only in the area of my church will I let Christ rule supreme in my life"— when in all other areas of your life your attitude is, "I'll take the reins from here, thank you."

On the other hand, if Jesus is truly the Lord of your individual life, then when you come together with others in the *church* setting, Jesus will be the same Lord corporately as He is individually. In other words, the way you revere and submit to Him in private is exactly the way you will revere and submit to Him in public.

He will rule. Or, "the people rule."

Plan A or Plan B.

There is no third choice.

And living in the final church age in which we do, the corporate personality, the combined integrity of the visible church will only be a reflection of the private righteousness, or personal lukewarmness, of the individual *called-out ones*.

Jesus knew all men.[7] Jesus saw the time in which we live. And what He saw was so distasteful, that He wanted to vomit us out of His mouth.[8]

What Am I To Do?

Joshua, as his life and ministry was drawing to a close, gave a final word of encouragement to the people of Israel. It was his final admonition to those who knew God and had been party to some of the greatest miracles ever recorded in the pages of Scripture. On that day, two separate, clearly defined, and divergent spiritual paths lay before them as individuals and as a nation.

It was to be a day of reckoning. It was their day to choose.

Joshua said, "If it is disagreeable in your sight to serve the Lord, choose for yourself today whom *YOU* will serve, whether the gods which your fathers served which are beyond the rivers or the gods of the Ammorites in whose land you are living, but as for *me* and *my* house (personal accountability to my own life and those who are under my authority) *we* will serve the Lord."[9]

When Joshua was giving this warning and plea to the people of God, his attitude was probably something like this, "Guys, I can't worry about what you do. You have to choose for yourself. But for me and my house, for me and those God has placed in my care, for me and my loved ones, we're going to serve the Lord. And we're going to serve Him whether you come with us or not. We're going to serve Him even if we have to do it alone."

Wouldn't it have been great if out of all the nation of Israel, Bobby would have jumped up and said, "But as for me and my house, I make the same commitment. I will serve the Lord, even if I have to do it alone. Hey, I'm with you, Joshua!"

Now there are two people ready to give all to the Lord— Joshua and Bobby.

Then Gary shouts from somewhere near the back of the crowd, "Hey, count me in." The number has now grown to three.

The sound of other voices begin to fill the air as one by one, like sprouting spring flowers, the children of Israel stood and took their *individual* stands for the Lord *together*.

Did you get that?

They took their "individual" stands for Christ "together".

Can you imagine the incredible national revival that would've taken place when each individual came and aligned themselves with the Lord and agreed with Joshua to allow Him to freely reign sovereign in their lives? As a result, all the disasters, the purging, judging, delivering, and devastation we read about in the Kings and Chronicles may have been avoided.

Well, maybe.

But that's not what happened.

In actuality, a lot of people stood and pledged, "Yeah, we're with you. From this day forward we will also serve the Lord only!" Yep, like the church today. They spoke the words with their mouths but didn't believe it with their hearts.

Kinda like us, wouldn't you say?

So, Whadda Ya Wanna Do?

So my question to each one of you is:

Do **you** believe the church can change society?

Do **you** believe the grace of God is stronger than anything Satan can throw at us?[10]

Do **you** believe the power of God is stronger than your apathy? How about stronger than my apathy or the apathy of others?

Do **you** want to be different? Uh, *really* different? Or, do **you** want to keep doing the same lifeless, boring, rote religious stuff over and over again that didn't work in the first place and then lie to yourself by saying it amounts to something important? Something spiritual?

Do **you** want to experience the *abundant life* Jesus promised us?[11]

Or, are **you** sadly satisfied with the status quo?

Do you love Jesus, yet find yourself loathing church?

Yeah, me too. Read on.

what we call normal, ain't normal

Victory is the normal experience of a Christian;
defeat should be the abnormal experience.
Watchman Nee from *The Normal Christian Life*

Over the last couple of chapters we've been talking about the Holy Spirit and the elusive, hard-to-define, abundant life in Christ that He has promised to each of us.

Remember?

Good. Then let's look at a couple of truths about *normal* Christianity you probably won't hear preached about this Sunday— or *any* Sunday for that matter.

The Two Kingdoms

First, each of us has a dual citizenship in two divergent, irreconcilable kingdoms.

On one hand, there's the kingdom of *this* world, the visible world, the world we experience with our own senses— with its own unique set of rules, regulations and realities. I'm sure you're probably *more* than a little familiar, maybe even comfortable, with this kingdom.

You should be. You've spent most of your life learning how to survive in it by playing by its rules.

It's the kingdom into which we were born and the kingdom we've spent most of our lives frantically striving to find its keys to success. It's literally the sum total of what we think we know *based* on what seems right to us…uh, *based* on what we've experienced in the past. Did you get all that?

It's classic Descartes, "I think, therefore I am."

It's the kingdom of "*my* rights, *my* wants, and *my* desires."

The kingdom of, "Hey, you hit me. Now I'm gonna hit you back… only harder."

It's the kingdom where the greatest among us is defined, not as one who serves, but as the one who *is* served by the weakest among us.

It's the kingdom made up of those who desperately want to control their own destiny and be the masters of their own lives— like the proverbial "picking one up by one's own bootstrap" thing. It's the kingdom of the "self-made man" cult.

I think you get the picture.

On the other hand, we have the Kingdom of God with all its illogical realities and strange truths that stretch and then defy human understanding.

In the Kingdom of God there's the unsettling notion that the greatest among us will become the servant of everyone else— uh, that's *willingly* become the servant of everyone else.[1] Whether they deserve it or not.

Sounds insane, doesn't it?

I know. But it's true.

Do you remember Jesus, the upper room, and the disciples' filthy feet?[2] Need I say more?

Then there's the troubling idea that we don't really belong in *this* world. That somehow we just don't fit. It's the idea we're stranded strangers, simple pilgrims, like modern day homeless people, just passing through on our way to another home— to our heavenly home. The home Jesus said He is now building for us in heaven.[3]

Heaven?

Nothing tangible. No brick and mortar. No long, winding driveways. Nothing we can see and show others. Nothing we can sink our teeth into.

We're on our trek to our *faith*-built heavenly home.

Geez! Be honest. Wouldn't it be nice to have some of *this* world's stuff while we're waiting to inhabit the heavenly home Jesus is preparing for us? Sometimes it's often hard to swallow when we face the injustices of this world.

Sometimes it doesn't seem fair.

But there's more.

There's the idea of joyfully giving to *everyone* who asks even if they don't seem to need it, or we don't feel like giving it, or if it takes away from what we think we might need ourselves.[4]

Then there's the command not to worry about what we will eat or drink or wear— or anything! Instead, we're to seek righteousness and the Kingdom of God first, above all else, and in return He has promised to take care of everything else in our lives.[5]

Whew. Let's face it, to the carnal, logical, analytical, and natural mind that makes no sense at all.

None.

I Know What You're Thinking

You're thinking, "Who in their right mind would work for 40 years at IBM just to retire in order to give his 401K to help meet the needs of someone he doesn't even like— or know, for that matter? Who would sit there and 'turn the other cheek' time and time again only to have it repeatedly slapped? That's ridiculous. Who would voluntarily take the unjust suffering of a wrong sitting down?[6] Who? To do nothing would border on abuse. It's sadomasochistic. It wouldn't be fair. I mean, isn't that why God created the legal profession? To help and protect us by making sure no one takes advantage of us?

"And, what's with this forgiveness thing? In this Kingdom of God I'm told to forgive someone who wrongs me continually.[7] Really? Now why in the world would I want to do that? Wouldn't it be smarter just to make sure I never let the person who needs my forgiveness be in a position to do something to me that would require me having to forgive him? After all, doesn't it say somewhere in the Bible, 'First time, shame on you. Second time, shame on me?'

"Is this what *this* Kingdom of God is speaking about? Or have we somehow got it all wrong?"

OK, do you feel better? Aren't you glad you got that off your chest? Good.

Now let's get back to the issue at hand.

Jesus and His Kingdom

We need to understand that Jesus constantly talked about His Kingdom— the Kingdom of God. It's almost like He was obsessed with the subject.

127

On one occasion Jesus said, "The kingdom of heaven is like a treasure hidden in the field, which a man found and hid again; and from *joy* over it he goes and sells *all* that he has and buys that field."[8] In other words, the Kingdom was of such great value that, for joy, the man sells everything this world holds dear to acquire the treasure of the Kingdom. And he does it with deep, satisfying joy— despite the stares or counsel of his family and friends to do otherwise. Why? Because this man found the joy *only* living in the Kingdom can bring.

Again, Jesus said "The kingdom of heaven is like a merchant seeking fine pearls, and upon finding one pearl of great value, he went and sold *all* that he had and bought it."[9]

Just one pearl.

Nothing more.

In essence, the merchant recognized the Kingdom was of more value than anything he had ever laid his eyes upon. Its allure was so intoxicating, so captivating, that nothing was going to deter him in his quest to possess so great a pearl. So much so, he was willing to give *all* he had for this one solitary pearl. Why? Because the merchant knew that *all* he had, or *all* he ever hoped to have in this world, paled in comparison to the Kingdom Jesus was offering.

It was chump change. Trinkets and trash.

Study the life and teachings of Jesus and you'll find He spent quite a bit of time and over a gallon of red ink talking, comparing, teaching, illustrating, and compelling others to embrace the Kingdom of God. But that's a subject we'll discuss in more detail in another chapter.

For now, the *one* truth we want to drive home is the simple fact that as Believers in Christ our citizenship is with Him, in His Kingdom— the Kingdom of God. The problem we all seem to have is a nagging tendency— no, more like an overpowering compulsion, to live in the kingdom of *this* world and walk away from the pearl of great wonder and immeasurable worth.

Torn Between Two Lovers…

The dilemma with most Christians is that, even though we claim to have received Jesus as our Lord and Savior and have tasted of the "abundant life" He spoke about (even if that taste is nothing more than a lick around the edge of the cup), we still foolishly choose to live in the kingdom of *this*

128

world and focus our lives on the present realities of something that has no eternal value. It's like a one-sided game of mental gymnastics we play with ourselves: We justify our carnality and our own fervency to have our own way by thinking we are a little better than we used to be, but not quite as good as we should be.

"But hey, that's okay. We're comfortable. And that's all that really matters, right?"

Wrong.

Scripture clearly states, "that friendship with the world is hostility toward God. Therefore whoever wishes to be a friend of the world makes himself an enemy of God."[10] Scripture goes on to say "the flesh sets its desire against the Spirit, and the Spirit against the flesh; for these are in opposition to one another."[11] In other words, the person who lives according to the Spirit is in dire contrast to the person who lives according to the flesh. And this contrast *promises* to lead to conflict. No, it's *guaranteed* to lead to conflict.

Major conflict.

After all, if the world hates you for living in His Kingdom— well, it hated Him first.[12]

Here's the problem.

The mental picture of our struggle in the Christian life that has unfortunately been preached from countless pulpits down through the years is that we are somehow caught between two compelling kingdoms and two compelling rulers— Jesus and Satan It's like being chained between two huge, irresistible forces, each greater than ourselves, that are relentlessly pulling us in different directions, demanding our attention and screaming for our allegiance.

You know, the old, "the things we want to do, we don't do, and the things that we don't want to do we do and oh, what a wretched man that I am caught between these two kingdoms."[13]

Caught powerless, impotent, and without hope.

Caught on this unending cycle of spiritual ups and downs, peaks and valleys, from adulation to apathy.

Oh, please.

Do we really believe that Jesus and Satan are somehow equals? Have we really bought into the lie that they somehow share the same power? Or, for that matter, the same Father?

The reality— the Truth, according to Scripture, is that Satan is *already* defeated.

He's busted.
De-fanged.
Neutered.
Whupped.
Dead meat.
Six feet under.
Taking a dirt nap.
I think you get the point.

As for you and I, we are currently positioned "in Christ" — and Christ is off the scale![14]

He's immeasurable.

Beyond comprehension.

Beyond what our human minds can even conceive.

Wow! I don't know about you, but that sounds pretty cool to me.

The curse of the casual, carnal Christian is that we don't live according to the truth we already know. We don't live anywhere close to the abundant life Jesus spoke about— the life found in the Kingdom of God. Oh, we can read about it. Talk about it. Maybe even long for it. But can we actually live it?

Want a sobering experience? Try reading the book of Acts. Read about the life the early church lived and fleshed out day by day, and then compare it with what you see in our churches every Sunday.

Notice any difference?

Yeah, me too.

Kind of embarrassing, isn't it?

Is it any surprise to you that millions of people **Love Jesus** and **Hate Church**?

If you're truly honest with yourself, the abundant life in Christ is *not* something most Believers today experience on an ongoing basis, like a permanent part of their lives. No, it's more like something we've heard about from others. Or, maybe we've experienced just enough of the Holy Spirit to know what we're missing. Remember the times in our lives when we felt and experienced the awesome, incredible, encompassing love of the Lord that took all our problems and cares away? The times when we were giddy with Him, joyously reveling in His goodness? The times when we heard His voice? Understood His command? Maybe felt His arms as they wrapped around us and held us tight like a loving father to his trusting child?

Ah, remember? Feels good to remember, doesn't it?

130

Feeling Like a Fool

Do you also remember our repeated experience, right after this Mount of Transfiguration time with the Lord that comes all too infrequently to each of us, the fleshy tendency of sin, drawing us like a strong current back into depression or old habits? Do you remember the "heights from which you have fallen", maybe time and time again?[15]

I do. And it hurts inside. Deep inside.

We've all experienced this flash and fade style of spiritually. It's pretty much the norm.

Hot today, cold tomorrow.

Some have reasoned, "Since I feel so guilty about being hot and then cold, maybe it would be better if I just stayed warm, lukewarm. Then I wouldn't feel so bad about myself."

Ah, lukewarm. Bad choice.

Scripture tells us a lukewarm Christian turns the Lord's stomach. Even makes Him sick. So much so that He literally vomits them out of His mouth. Splat![16]

Sound crude? Well, take it up with Him. I'm just telling you what He said.

In our culture, in the land of the shadowy grey, the politically correct, the ever-changing relative truth, we preach this anemic, flash and fade Christian walk as a Biblical given— as the Normal Christian life. Preachers continually tell their congregations that they are just "ol' sinners saved by grace and hanging on by their fingertips until the rapture comes." Why would they say such a thing? And why in the world would we sit passively and listen to this kind of religious crap? Simple. It affirms and validates our experience and makes our half-hearted, anemic stab at the Christian life seem like the norm— like the Normal Christian life. And if lukewarmness is defined as normal, well...then there's really nothing wrong with us and there is nothing more we could do to make our Christian life, uh...er...more like Christ.

"Hey, we tried. Gave it our best shot. It's not our fault. We're *normal*, just like everybody else."

And it feels good to be told that we're just like everybody else, doesn't it?

But I don't see that in Scripture. Do you?

In Scripture I see the spiritual life as a walk from infancy to maturity, being all the more conformed to His image with each step we take. It's like we're all on this path to Christlikeness, living one day at a time. Some of us run, some of us walk— but we're all heading in the same direction, following the same Lord, blessed to be bearing His fruit. Sure, we may stumble and fall on the way. But stumbling into sin and apathy is *not* the *normal* Christian life as revealed in Scripture. It's the exception to the rule— and *not* the rule itself. It acts against the Spirit Jesus left with each of us.

It's just not normal.

No. Normal Christianity, from the Bible's perspective, is something quite different. Quite different, indeed.

Hey, Who You Calling Normal?

I'm firmly convinced the "normal" Christian life *is* the *abundant* Christian life.

Jesus said He came to "give us life and give it to the fullest— to give it abundantly."[17] He didn't say He was going to let us hang around in the muck and mire hoping in vain for some sort of victory in our lives He reserved only for His favorites— you know, those select few who somehow meet some standard or do something magnanimous.

No, I believe it's almost like we all start with the fulfillment of the promise, the abundant life in Christ. Then we, by our own fleshly actions, disqualify ourselves from something that is really our inheritance and really belongs to us.

It's not like we have to strive to get there. It's like we had it all the time and, for some stupid reason, just turned our backs on it and walked away.

Arrgh! Like how stupid is that? We must be brain-dead morons.

Stupid Bumper Stickers

So what are we to do? How do we live the Normal Christian life as defined by Scripture and not the normal Christian life as portrayed by the church? How do we exist in the Kingdom of God and not in the kingdom of the flesh— the kingdom of this world?

Great question. Are you ready for a great answer?

It all has to do with the proclamation of popular truths we internalize everyday. They feel good in this kingdom and agree with our flesh so…hey, why not?

We see them portrayed on the car bumpers of well-meaning Christians who believe, in a misguided sort of way, that it's a silent witness to the goodness of God. A testimony to Him. An evangelical tool.

Ha. What a joke.

Not sure what I'm talking about?

Ok, have you ever seen one of these bumper stickers? Do you have one on your car?

"Christians Aren't Perfect, Just Forgiven."
Or, worse than that, **"God is My Co-Pilot."**

Let's take the first one first, and you'll quickly begin to see why people, just like you, are finally realizing that it's okay to **Love Jesus** and **Hate Church**.

holy crap!— and other sermons by frank barone

"Holy, Holy, Holy, is the Lord of hosts.
The whole earth is full of His glory!"
From the account of Isaiah, confirmed by John

"Holy smoke!"
"Holy Toledo!"
"Holy mackerel!"
"Holy crap!"
You know, that's just about as close to true holiness as much of the church will ever get.

Think about it for a moment.
When Isaiah in the Old and John in the New Testament caught a glimpse of the Father in His Glory, do you remember what they saw? They saw the four living creatures that surround His throne proclaim, 24/7, the *single* attribute that's most like God. The *one* supreme attribute that's most descriptive of Him. And it's not love or longsuffering or patience or grace or mercy or any of the other character traits we sing about every Sunday, *ad infinitum*.

No, the definitive, descriptive attribute of God is *holiness*.

The four living creatures cry out day and night for all eternity...
"Holy, Holy, Holy is the Lord of Hosts!"

Ah, holiness— His pure, unadulterated holiness.

Holiness— the one attribute of God that is conspicuously absent in our modern, enlightened, watered-down brand of Christianity.

Oh, once again, do you think I'm a tad bit too dogmatic? Am I bringing my shotgun to a knife fight? Have I offended you again? Geez.

So you want proof? Ok, read on.

Licking the Edge of the Cup

For years I've been asking the Lord what He requires to live the kind of life I see portrayed in Scripture— you know, the kind of life we all secretly desire but have convinced ourselves is just beyond our grasp. What must I do to live in the fullness of the Lord that I see fleshed-out in the lives of the prophets or in the sold-out life of the early church? What do *they* have that I don't? What's missing?

What is the key to the *abundant life* that Jesus talked about?[1]

Now the current, feel-good, TV-style Christianity would try to sell me on the fact that I haven't sowed enough of *my* funds into *their* ministry in order to reap the harvest of unbroken intimacy with the Father. Really? I didn't know there was a connection between the two. Seems kind of self-serving to me.

"You give Benny a dollar and God will reward you with a blessing."

Hey, God's got to. Benny said so.

I wonder if the concept is transferable? Will it also work for Jessie, Paul and Jan, Paula, Joel or the myriad of religious perverts who want to put their hands down my pants and fondle my wallet?

I wonder.

Others would tell me that I have to "rebuke that foul spirit of…well, *something*" and purchase their Holy Land Anointing Oil in order to break through to intimacy with the Lord. Oh, and that intimacy *always* comes packaged with cars, houses, cash, and wealth beyond my wildest dreams. After all, they reason, the first thing the Lord wants to do when I come into His presence is load me down with stuff… you know, like a cosmic Santa Clause. He just wants to make my life easier and more blessed in the world that the Bible states is not my home.[2]

Yeah, right.

It's amazing that the pundits of today feel they have to couple intimacy with God with trinkets and toys to make it seem more attractive. As if intimacy with the Father was somehow second rate— like the consolation prize given to the loser.

"And if you call within the next five minutes we'll give you as an added bonus, *Intimacy with God*! All you have to do is pay for shipping and handling."

So it's buy the book, listen to the tape, attend the conference, pray the prayer, repeat the affirmation, write the check, or touch the "point of contact" and soon you'll be on your way to the life of luxury— the abundant life Jesus promised to those that belong to Him.

What a crock of crap!

Or Taking a Big Gulp

Looking for truth, I began asking the Lord a couple of questions.

"Lord, what is it that You require?"

"What truly pleases You?"

Come on, you know you've asked the Lord the same questions. After all, isn't that what we all really want? Isn't that why we come to church each Sunday?

Let's face it, we *know* who Jesus is— He is, as Paul wrote to Timothy, the Son of God that has come into the world to save sinners.[3]

We *know* what Jesus has done— He has redeemed us, He has saved us, He has empowered us, and He is even now preparing a place for us to be where He is.

We *know* the Holy Spirit lives within us. The book of Ephesians says He is our deposit and guarantee for our inheritance to come.[4]

Yeah, we *know* all that!

But what we really want to *know* is the all-encompassing joy of being used by Him— to be the glove in which His hand is moving. Sometimes we've tasted it. Sometimes we've licked the cup of His presence. But most of the time we haven't really experienced Him in the way we see in Scripture. We haven't thrown our head back and taken a big gulp of the Lord.

For me, I've personally experienced a lot of good people doing a lot of good things— but very little of the power of God moving like He did in the book of Acts. And I have to wonder why.

Why did He use the Apostle Paul the way He did? Why Peter? Why the early church?

Why them?

Which leads to the even more troubling questions: Why not me? Why not us? Why not the church today?

There are *many* reasons why God doesn't move today in the midst of the contemporary church like He did in the past. Many reasons.

Do you want to know one of the biggest?

Good. Then hang with me for a couple of pages and we'll look at our addiction to Bumper Sticker Theology.

Christians Aren't Perfect, Just Forgiven

Have you ever seen this popular bumper sticker on the back of a mini-van, SUV, or a beat-up old Chevy? Sure you have. In fact, you may even have one on your own car.

Got a quick question for you: Why?

What's the point of this bit of pop theology? What are we trying to say with this statement? What direction are we heading with this lethal dose of feel-good pabulum?

Christians Aren't Perfect, Just Forgiven. What does this statement really mean? What are we really trying to say? Are we basing our theology on our personal experience as lukewarm Christians or basing it on the power of the Word of God?[5] Have we come to the conclusion that since we can't seem to get even close to leading *"perfect"* lives then…well, uh…I guess we're just not supposed to?[6] It's just not in the cards. Living imperfect, sinful lives must be what Jesus expects from us. It must be His will. So what's the point of trying to be different?

After all, isn't that why we're **Just Forgiven**?

Give me a break!

To be brutally honest, this Bumper Sticker theological statement is nothing more than our public license to sin. It's our excuse for *not* living holy, sanctified, Christ-like lives. It's our precious **Get Out Of Hell Free Card** that states we can live like we want simply because **Christians Aren't Perfect, Just Forgiven**. It's the popular doctrine of demons that tells us it's okay to live in sin— just as long as we've prayed some lame prayer that's guaranteed to bring us kicking and screaming, like spoiled, rebellious children, into a relationship with God.[7]

A *Holy* God, may I add.

"Oh, I'm sorry. My mistake. Gosh, I sinned again. But hey, I'm not perfect…just *forgiven*." Hence, I'll sin again and again and again with no compulsion to ever rise above the moral cesspool of acceptable Laodicean Christian behavior.[8]

And you wonder why people **Love Jesus** and **Hate Church**!

Please understand, before we go any further, that God is not One to take His holiness for granted. He's not One who winks, smiles, and turns a blind eye to the willful, premeditated sin and rebellion in His children. He's not the kind of parent who shrugs the shoulder and says, "Gosh, boys will be boys" and lets sinful behavior continue.

Never has. Never will.

This false concept of God's nature as only "grace, grace, grace" flies in the face of the "glorious gospel of the blessed God" that Paul spoke about to Timothy.[9] It's an incomplete rendering of the very nature of the Father designed to make His children feel comfortable in their disobedience. And Scripture shows us He's *very* concerned that His children reflect His nature— His holiness.

Want some examples? Ok, try these on for size.

The Nature of God and His Children

The Holy Spirit: Read that again. Slowly. Out loud.

Did you notice anything *holy* about the name of the Third Person of the Trinity? Like, duh? It's Holy Spirit. The *Holy* Spirit. It's not the Merciful Spirit. Or the Loving Spirit. Or the Spirit of Grace, or of Longsuffering, or Patience, or Forgiveness or whatever other attribute of God we want to push to the forefront.

No, the single attribute that describes God the Spirit is the same single, primary, all-important attribute that describes God the Father— Holiness.

So if God the Father and God the Son and God the (Holy) Spirit are holy— what does that say about His desire for His children to reflect His nature?

"Ah," slap hand on forehead. "I coulda had a V8!"

Maybe that's why Jesus said, "Therefore you are to be *perfect*, as your heavenly Father is *perfect*."[10]

Or as Peter echoed, "As obedient children, do not be conformed to the former lusts which were yours in your ignorance, but like the Holy One who called you, *be holy yourselves* also in *all your behavior*; because it is written, 'You shall be *holy*, for I am *holy*.'"[11]

Saints: In the New Testament, Believers in Christ are called *saints*.

"Saints? Naw! Can't be."

Ah, but it is.

Listen how Paul speaks in his letters to the various churches:

Romans: "to all who are beloved of God in Rome, called as *saints*."[12]

1 Corinthians: "to the church of God which is at Corinth, to those who have been sanctified in Christ Jesus, *saints* by calling."[13]

2 Corinthians: "to the church of God which is at Corinth with all the *saints* who are throughout Achaia."[14]

Ephesians: "I pray that the eyes of your heart may be enlightened, so that you may know what is the hope of His calling, what are the riches of the glory of His inheritance in the *saints*, and what is the surpassing greatness of His power towards us who believe."[15]

Philippians: "All the *saints* greet you, especially those of Caesar's household."[16]

Colossians: "to the *saints* and faithful brethren in Christ who are at Colossae."[17]

Get the point? When Paul talked about the church, the living Body of Christ, he referred to them as *saints*.

Now when you and I think of the word *saints*, we often tend to think of the larger-than-life religious figures who, against incredible odds, accomplished great things for God. We think of people whose pictures adorn stained-glass windows or who fill the illustrated pages in our Bibles. We think of Saint Paul or Saint Peter or maybe the likes of Saint Augustine or Saint Francis of Assisi— all these over-the-top, sold-out Christian icons that somehow met some illusive spiritual standard we can never meet. But for some reason, we never associate the word *saint* with Saint Frank the auto repair guy or Saint Judy the hairstylist.

That's too human. Too obtainable. Way too close to home.

By the way, do you know what the term *saints* means?

You got it: "*holy ones*."

When the Scriptures call us *saints*, or *holy ones*, it is calling us by the very nature of the God we are to reflect in our very lives. It's calling us by the name of the Spirit that inhabits us— we were "sealed in Him with the Holy Spirit of promise, who is given as a pledge of our inheritance in Him."[18]

Now, let's read it again.

Romans: "to all who are beloved of God in Rome, called as *holy ones*."

1 Corinthians: "to the church of God which is at Corinth, to those who have been sanctified in Christ Jesus, *holy ones* by calling."

2 Corinthians: "to the church of God which is at Corinth with all the *holy ones* who are throughout Achaia."

Ephesians: "I pray that the eyes of your heart may be enlightened, so that you may know what is the hope of His calling, what are the riches of the glory of His inheritance in the *holy ones*, and what is the surpassing greatness of His power towards us who believe."

Philippians: "All the *holy ones* greet you, especially those of Caesar's household."

Colossians: "to the *holy ones* and faithful brethren in Christ who are at Colossae."

We, on the other hand, tend to view ourselves as just old sinners saved by grace, hanging on by our fingertips until the rapture comes.

Wow! Can you see how believers who excuse sin and hold onto "grace, grace, grace" could lead others to **Love Jesus** and **Hate Church**?

Just a few more from the Old Testament and we'll call it a chapter.

<u>**The Nature of God**</u>: God demanding that we reflect His nature:

"For I am the LORD who brought you up from the land of Egypt to be your God; thus you shall be *holy*, (why) for *I am holy*."[19]

Then the LORD spoke to Moses, saying: "Speak to all the congregation of the sons of Israel and say to them, 'You shall be holy, (why) for *I the LORD your God am holy*'."[20]

"You shall consecrate yourselves therefore and be holy, (why) for *I am the LORD your God*. You shall keep My statutes and practice them; (why) *I am the LORD who sanctifies you*."[21]

Oh, then there are the Scriptures that show God's commitment to prove Himself holy among His people and to vindicate the holiness of His name. As a sample, let's look at a couple of verses in Ezekiel:

> Therefore say to the house of Israel, "Thus says the Lord GOD, It is not for your sake, O house of Israel, that I am about to act, but for *My holy name*, which you have profaned among the nations where you went. *I will vindicate the holiness of My great name* which has been profaned among the nations, which you have profaned in their midst. Then the nations will know that I am the LORD," declares the Lord GOD, "when *I prove Myself holy* among you in their sight."[22]

Finally, we see God telling His creation how it's going to be. Intimidating.

> "For from the rising of the sun even to its setting, *My name will be great among the nations*, and in every place incense is going to be offered to My name, and a grain offering that is pure; for *My name will be great among the nations*," says the LORD of hosts.[23]

Anyway, have you had enough? Are you beginning to see how important holiness is to God and how unimportant it is to His church? Do you understand we cannot live in the shadows and still claim to have fellowship and intimacy with God in the light?

As John so clearly puts it:

"If we say that we have fellowship with Him and yet walk in the darkness, we *lie* and do not practice the truth."[24]

The Precursor to Holiness

I was considering all that you've read and my desire for a deeper relationship with the Lord and I began to wonder: What's the precursor to holiness? I mean, there has to be one! What's the core, the key thread that runs through the lives of those who have experienced face-to-face intimacy with the Father? What trait or attribute does God look for in a believer that leads to the abundant life in Christ we all desire but aren't disciplined enough to partake of?

I think I've found it. Are you ready?

The precursor to holiness is actually something harder to come to grips with than the single attribute of God we spend hours trying to blow off and not feel guilty about. Truth be told, I've never heard much contemporary preaching on the subject. I certainly didn't have it taught to me in seminary, and I have yet to see a number of books on the subject making the New York Times Bestseller list. In fact, I don't ever remember seeing *one* book on this key requirement for the holiness that brings intimacy with God. Oh, there are a lot of books about me— *10 Steps to a Happy Marriage* or *How to Get Your Guardian Angel to Work for You*, ad nauseam kind of stuff, but there's a literal famine on the Christian bookshelf of books that teach about God's desire for holiness in His people, let alone His church.

So what's the answer? What's the precursor to a life of holiness?

I'll let the Lord tell you from His own lips. It's pretty simple, really.

Jesus asks the pointed question, "Why do you call me Lord, Lord, and not do the things I tell you?"[25]

Good question. Do we have a good answer?

Then, as Jesus is telling His disciples about the coming of the Holy Spirit (remember Him from above), He clearly establishes the requirements for receiving this incredible gift.

Notice the implication of the simple, *if*.

> "*If* you love Me, (what) *you will keep My commandments*. I will ask the Father, and He will give you another Helper, that He may be with you forever; that is the Spirit of truth, whom the world cannot receive, because it does not see Him or know Him, but you know Him because He abides with you and will be in you."[26]

Did you catch the power of His words?

If you love Me, you will show that love by keeping My commandments. Come on, how simple can it get? No rocket science here! We expect it from our kids— how much more should Jesus expect it from us?

Then to drive the point home even further, Jesus adds:

> "He who has My commandments and (what) *keeps them* is the one who loves Me; and he who loves Me will be loved by My Father, and I will love him and will (what) *disclose Myself to him*."[27]

Or, to put it another way: He who obeys Me shows himself to be the one who loves Me. And, as a result, I will love Him and have intimacy with Him.

The key: Obedience.
The result: Holiness.
The reward: Intimacy.

Now, turn the page and let's take a closer look at this concept of obedience and see how it relates to those who **Love Jesus** and **Hate Church**.

Please, after you.

.

"hey, I coulda been a contender!"

"Do or do not do…there is no try."
Yoda, *Star Wars*

Are you an old movie buff? Boy, I am. Anything in black and white gets my attention.

This is from one of my favorites.

Terry (Marlon Brando): It wasn't him. It was you, Charley. You and Johnny. Like the night the two of youse come in my dressin' room and says "kid, it ain't your night... we're going for the price on Wilson." It ain't my night, Charley! I woulda taken Wilson apart that night! I was ready—remember the early rounds throwin' them combinations?

So what happens? This bum Wilson gets the title shot— outdoors in the ballpark! And what do I get? A couple of bucks and a one way ticket to Palookaville. It was you, Charley. You was my brother, you should've looked out for me 'stead of makin' me take them dives for the short end money.

Charley (Rod Steiger): I always had a bet down for you. You saw some money.

Terry: See! You don't understand!

Charley: I tried to keep you in good with Johnny.

Terry: You don't understand, Charley, I coulda had class and been somebody. Real class. I coulda been a contenda 'stead of a bum! Let's face it, that's what I am.

from *On the Waterfront*

Pride.

The original sin.

The curse of mankind and the greatest tool of the flesh in its relentless campaign against the spirit.

Hold on for a minute. Let's catch our breath and take a quick break. I don't know about you, but I feel the need to regroup a bit.

It seems that we've droned on for page after page examining the life we are to live in Christ and showing, in vivid, no-holds-barred details, the total failure of much of what we call church to live up to that standard or to even *care* about living up to the standard we see in Scripture. We've tried through **Love Jesus**, **Hate Church** to faithfully echo the command of Jesus to His church to "remember the heights from where you have fallen and repent and do the things you did at first."[1]

Only time will tell how those for whom Christ died will receive our message.

It's much like the parable of the sower and the soils. Remember? Some seeds fell on the hard, prideful path and the enemy came and snatched them up before they could take root and produce a crop. And yet others fell on fertile soil and produced a bountiful harvest some 100, 60 and 40 fold.[2] The determining factor of success in the parable was *not* the quality of the seed or the skill of the one sowing. No, the factor that determines success or failure is the simple condition of the soil— the openness of one's heart to the message of Christ.

And quite honestly, the success or failure of **Love Jesus**, **Hate Church** will also be determined by the condition of *your* heart— your willingness to read and receive hard truth.

Truth, by the way, that may make you feel uncomfortable. Uneasy.

Truth that may assault your sense of well-being, maybe even your sense of satisfaction with your spiritual life and your relationship with the church.

In essence, truth that may hurt your pride— your confidence in all you hold to be good and true and real.

Are you ready? Sure hope so.

Question: What's the condition of your heart to receive troubling truth? Are you traveling on a pride path? Or are you living in an open, fertile field?

Answer: I guess only time will tell.

So, if you don't mind, let's just cut to the chase with this chapter and dive in for the kill like a Great White. The issue of pride and self-exaltation, and the damning effect it has had on the church, the **Well-Oiled Machine**, needs no introduction. There's no need to "set the scene" or "put the reader in the picture," as they say. Naw.

That's just a waste of time and print.

Let's just dive right in, shall we?

Bumper Sticker Theology Revisited

Ah, remember from the last chapter our fascination with Bumper Sticker theology?

First, there was our public license to sin:

Christians Aren't Perfect, Just Forgiven

And now, our blatant declaration that God was created in *our* image. He works for *us*. He's *our* ever-present Genie in a Bottle— always ready to do *our* bidding, no matter how selfish and self-centered that bidding may be:

God is *My* Co-Pilot

Ugh!

Have you ever seen this slogan pasted on the bumper of an automobile or stacked in racks with the other Christian Evangelistic Tools in Christian bookstores beckoning to be bought as part of our misguided *Witness While You Drive* fulfillment of the Great Commission?

Sure you have. Well, I've got a couple of questions for you.

Question: What are we trying to say with this bit of Bumper Sticker Theology? What message are we trying to communicate to the world about our relationship with the very Lord to whom we're attempting to introduce them?

What does **God is *My* Co-Pilot** really mean?

What's the logical conclusion, the guaranteed outcome of a life filled with the attitude that says, "God, I'll take it from here. You be ready just in case I need You to bail me out again. Until then, move over and let *me* drive."

Answer: Oh, that's easy. It leads to a life of disobedience.

The *anti*-precursor to holiness.

Think about it, God's desire for us as His children is to be holy, first and foremost.

Above anything else.

Without reservation.

No living in the shadows.

Remember? We talked about that in the chapter titled, *Holy Crap*.

Jesus said we are to be "*perfect* as our heavenly Father is *perfect*."[3] In other words, we are to be like God. We are to reflect His glory and His nature.

Then, when we take an honest look at our contemporary church culture and the lukewarm examples of its leaders, we come to the conclusion that it's impossible for us to be perfect and to live the holy lives God demands. There's just no way we can be like God or reflect His nature.

No way, no how, nada, *neet*!

Why? Because the very ones we look up to— our pastors, evangelists, teachers, parents, leaders, and mentors seem to be quite comfortable living in the gray areas of lukewarm spiritual apathy. And if *they* can't seem to live holy and perfect lives in Christ— well, then there's no hope for any of us. It must be impossible to be like Christ.

And since it's impossible to be like Him— well, why try?

As Charlie Brown would say, "We're doomed."

Really?

If that's true, then I guess it means Jesus commanded us to do something He never empowered us to do. It means Jesus gave us a standard to live by, to be judged by, and then for some perverted, cruel reason made it impossible for us to reach. Sounds incredibly frustrating to me. Not stuff the *abundant life* in Christ is all about.[4]

Again, really?

The Scriptures state that "God is light and in Him there is no darkness at all."[5] Ok, we can buy that. No problem there. But then it goes on to say that "If we claim to have fellowship with the light (with God as one of His children), but walk in darkness (live a life of non-perfection— in the gray areas) *we lie* and do not practice the truth."[6]

Uh-oh. Now it gets a bit sticky. The Word of God has taken away my place to hide, my place to sin in secret.

The truth, as revealed in 1 John 1, states that if I claim to love Jesus and yet continue to sin, I'm a hypocrite and a liar and don't practice what I claim to believe as truth.

Ouch! Kinda stings, doesn't it?

I'm either lying about loving Jesus or I'm lying about being in the *light*— in the Truth. I'm lying about being His.

There is no third curtain. No Monty's Cookie Jar.[7]

The Lesser of Two Lies

So now I'm faced with a troubling dilemma. One, I must admit that I truly don't love the Lord as much as I claim I do. I must confess that I have no problem sticking my fist in His face and saying, "No way! I'll not obey You, Jesus. And You can't make me!"

Or, I have to admit that I'm not really His— and I'm not really "born again" or "saved" or "redeemed by the blood of the Lamb" or whatever else you want to call it. I have to simply own up to the fact that I'm lost and deceived and that my salvation experience was nothing more than an emotional one at best. That, as the Scripture states, I have a "form of godliness but devoid of any life changing power."[8]

I'm one of the ones to whom Jesus would say:

> "Not everyone who says to Me, 'Lord, Lord,' will enter
> the kingdom of heaven, but he who *does the will of
> My Father* who is in heaven will enter. Many will say
> to Me on that day, 'Lord, Lord, did we not prophesy in
> Your name, and in Your name cast out demons, and in
> Your name perform many miracles?' And then I will
> declare to them, 'I never knew you; depart from Me,
> (who) you who *practice lawlessness.*'"[9]

"Uh, I'm stunned. Isn't there a third option?"

Sure is. But you're not going to like that one either.

"Ok," you reason, "I don't want to believe that my love for the Lord is false or self-serving or lame at best. No, that's unsettling. So, I'll nix option one to explain my love for sin. But I can't accept the fact that I may have been deceived all these years, and that salvation is something more than the three-lined prayer I prayed with all my friends at the close of VBS that summer when I was twelve. That's even more unsettling. So I'll have to big time nix option two to explain my gray area living.

"Where do I go from here?"

Option Three: Simple, you can let the pride of life and the lust of self-love move in and drown out the obedience and allegiance you owe the Lord. You can become the lord of your life and, therefore, choose to obey or disobey Christ's command at will— without a tinge of guilt. How? By demoting God to the second chair, to the backseat, to the thankless job of being *your* co-pilot. You can proclaim to the world that **God is *My* Co-Pilot**. Which, by the way, makes *you* the god of your life and God not much more than the pinch hitter.

"Impossible!" you say.

Ah, we do it all the time.

For example, the Scriptures state, "Therefore, having these promises, beloved, let us cleanse ourselves from all defilement of flesh and spirit, *perfecting holiness* in the fear of God."[10]

Then, "As obedient children, do not be conformed to the former lusts which were yours in your ignorance, but like the Holy One who called you, *be holy yourselves* also in *all your behavior*; because it is written, 'You shall be holy, for I am holy.'"[11]

So how do we handle these commands from the Lord when stacked up against our lust for sin? How do we reconcile the two? Where is the middle ground— the *balance*, as we are so fond of saying?

The Big Sins

First, we pride ourselves on our supposed victory over the **Big Sins**. Or, **BS** for short.

Let's take Joe's life as an example. He's happily married to his wife, so he's not going to have an affair or commit adultery. Hurray for Joe!

He views himself as an *honest* Christian person— so he's not going to steal. Why? Well, it would be out of character for him to do so and he doesn't particularly relish the thought of getting caught.

Joe tries to control his anger so he won't snap and kill somebody with an ice pick, or run them over with a garden tiller. He's made it a practice to speak the truth whenever he can and, to the best of his knowledge, he doesn't lie. Uh, except for the little one he just told when he said he doesn't lie. Actually, that was a lie.

"I think I lied about not lying," Joe would say. "No, really. It's true. I'm not lying. Well, kinda, sorta."

Anyway, based on Joe's supposed victory over the **BS** in his life, he'll naturally come to the conclusion that he must be pretty holy and righteous, you know *Top Dog* in his own estimation of his spiritual life. Why? Because he doesn't do those terrible sins that other people do.

"Hey, I'm okay. Resting easy. Just my self-righteousness and me."

Sound familiar? Have you ever met Joe? I'll bet you have. How about the last time you looked in the mirror?

Ok, so Joe and the millions of other Christians that hold on to this third option of self-justification feel pretty smug with the bit of victory they've tasted with the last six of the Ten Commandments. Remember them? They're the ones that deal with our horizontal relationships. They govern our interactions with each other.

"But what about the first four?"

Oh, now that's a different subject altogether. A horse of a different color.

Let's see: I'm to love the Lord with all my heart, mind and soul. I'm to love the Lord with all that I am— all that I ever hope to be. I'm not to have any other god in my life. None. I'm to honor His name, His glory, His day— everything about Him. Always![12] Or, as John puts it in such practical terms, "I'm to live in the light where He is in the light. Where there's no darkness at all."[13]

Anything less than that is… well, it's sin!

What's So Personal About Personal Holiness?

"But, that's a personal issue— my *personal* holiness. You can't put requirements or standards on me or my behavior because that would be intolerant. You'd be judging me. Right? And that'd be wrong. Right?"

Well, let's see.

For years we've heard it preached that we needed to examine our *personal holiness* in regards to the mandates of Scripture to see how we're doing and how we're measuring up to being Christ-like. We put the word *personal* in front of holiness because *personal* means that it's a personal, private, individual matter.

Which translated means: **Don't Ask** and **Don't Tell**.

It devalues the commands of obedience in Scripture.

"Hey, I won't look at your life *if* you won't look at mine. Then we can both wallow in the lukewarm gray muck and not feel guilty— or dirty. Whadayathink? Works for me if it works for you!"

The Bottom Line— the Choice

The bottom line is this— we have a choice.

We can be a member of the **Well-Oiled Machine** just like everybody else and rock along smiling in our self-satisfied aura that says, "I'm OK and You're OK and God loves us just fine." And by American church standards you can feel pretty darn spiritual judging yourself by yourself.

For example, I remember my dad telling me years ago when I asked him how he reconciled his supposed love for Christ with his movie viewing habits (he loved to watch the R-rated, sexual, slasher movies.). His answer was just as sick as his movie viewing preference. But not unlike those same excuses I've heard from others in church to justify their lukewarm, gray area, non-holy living.

"You see son," he would begin, patronizingly. "Before I got saved I was 95% bad and 5% good. Now that I've become a Christian, I'm 85% good and Jesus lets me have the other 15%."

Really? Heave. Gag. Vomit. Splat!

Give me a break!

Look, you can homeschool your kids, go to church a couple times a week, put the little fish sign on the backside of your car, read your Bible and devotional book daily, tithe, serve as a deacon or an elder or Sunday school teacher or a youth leader or…whatever! You can do all sorts of good things that make you, by your own standards, feel like a real pinnacle, over-the-top, "I'm better-than-you" Christian.

And if it's less than true obedience to the Lord, your righteousness amounts to nothing more than *filthy rags*.[14] Or, to put that passage in its literal form "used menstrual cloths." Huh? Oh yeah. Our righteousness is just a big pile of used Kotex pads or soiled tampons. Arrgh!

I know, heave, gag, vomit and splat! Again.

Or you can say, with the heroes of Hebrews 11, "No, I want more. I want the intimate life with Jesus I've seen modeled in Scripture. I want what I've read about in the autobiographies of great heroes of the faith like Corrie Ten Boom and D.L. Moody. I want what they had— only more! I want to be totally surrendered to Him. I want Him to be Lord over my future, my reputation, my job, my family, my thought life— everything!

"I want Jesus be my Lord, 24/7. I want to give Him all that I am. I want to live in His kingdom. I want to live a holy and righteous life— you know, to reflect His glory. I want to obey Him no matter what.

"I want to be the kind of worshiper the Father seeks worship from.[15] Oh yeah, I want to be just like Jesus."

Really? Are you serious?
If so, then what's the excuse? What's the deal?

Simple.
Turn the page and let's discover the single truth that determines obedience and undermines pride. Or, at the very least, let's see that truth in a new light.
Again, after you.

burger king, french fries and the kingdom of god

"Going to church doesn't make you a Christian anymore than going to McDonalds makes you a hamburger."

"I repent of ever having recorded one single song, and ever having performed one concert, if my music, and more importantly, my life has not provoked you into Godly jealousy or to sell out more completely to Jesus!"
Keith Green (1954-1982)

The Place: Burger King
The Time: A little after the lunch rush.
The Characters: One harried woman and two small children.
The Props: French fries, ketchup and a stained shirt.

Let me tell you about an experience I had not long ago.

I'm sitting at Burger King, minding my own business, nursing a Diet Coke and watching the noontime herd of people mindlessly file in to eat. They were an assorted lot— construction workers with mud-caked boots, car salesmen with large bellies, white shirts and small black ties and, of course, the band of tired mothers with a string of small children in tow. One after another they'd belly up to the bar, slap down a twenty and say, "Whoppers, fries and Kid's Meals all around."

What catches my eye, however, is this intriguing scene that's being played out two tables to my right.

Let me see if I can describe the characters to you.

First, there was **The Woman**: Shoulders slumped, head buried in her hands— depressed, detached, just going through the motions, her mind focused *anywhere* other than where she was. She looked to be in her mid-thirties, maybe. It was hard to tell. Her youth and joy must've been swallowed up by whatever caused the years of deep sadness that were etched on her face. I can't imagine what was going on in her life but whatever it was, it didn't look good.

Actually, it was kind of sad.

Then, seated on each side of her were her two small children, a boy and a girl, blissfully eating French fries.

Next, **The Boy**: By the looks of him he seemed to be about five. And, by the grin on his face, you would of thought he had died and gone to heaven. He was in ecstasy, French fries stuffed in both hands — like a newlywed on his honeymoon. Every time he would slam a fry in his mouth his face would break into a wide grin that said, "Look at me, I'm at Burger King! I'm with my mom. I'm eating my French fries and this is *soooo* cool. Life doesn't get any better than this!" He would smile at his sister and his sister would smile back. Giggling. Fry after fry. Why? It's the joy, the journey— just childlike faith having a great time eating French fries.

Finally, **The Red Comma**: And as fate would have it, a triple-dipped fry with a big wad of ketchup dangling from the end broke off and tumbled down the front of his white, Winnie the Pooh, shirt. Splat! The boy looked down at his shirt. Then he looked up at his mom. Time stood still. Finally, with a determined, "I can fix this" expression on his face, he grabbed a handful of napkins and tried to wipe the ketchup off his shirt leaving behind a smear that looked something like a large, red comma. But hey! He didn't care. He was having a good time.

"Look at me, I'm at Burger King! I'm with my mom. I'm eating my French fries and this is *soooo* cool. Life doesn't get any better than this!"

Ignoring the comma, he went right back to dipping those French fries again.

His sister was so excited about it.

And for the rest of the day *anyone* who came across this kid would see the tell-tale evidence of how much fun he had at Burger King.

Oh, and his mother? Well, she looked like she was about to cry.

Slowly she exhaled, looked up and just rolled her eyes. One more unbearable burden for her to bear.

Sigh.

So what made the mother and the child view the same situation differently? Why did a simple red punctuation mark bring excitement to the boy, and tired resignation to the mother? Why did a stained Pooh shirt bring tears of grief to one, and tears of joy to another? After all, it was just ketchup. Yet sometimes we act as if it was blood.

Why? Simple. The same reasons that prompt some of us to **Love Jesus** and **Hate Church**.

The Kingdom of God

Sometimes we miss the greatest blessings because of the simple irritants in life. And sometimes we miss the greatest blessings in life because *we* are the simple irritants.

The standard joke in Christian circles is that the life with Christ is anything but abundant. No, it's more like riding a giant roller coaster at Six Flags. We stand in awe and expectation at the gate to the Georgia Cyclone waiting on our turn for "the time of our life."

We're strapped in tight. We wave to our friends. And the ride begins.

Up and down. Round and round. Rightside up and upside down. Shaking our insides. Filling us with sheer excitement and then— sheer terror.

And when the ride finally comes to an end— we feel queasy and want to throw up. Swearing we'll never do *that* again!

Ah, the *abundant life* of the contemporary Christian.[1]

But you know, it's just not supposed to be that way.

Our life with Christ is supposed to be so wonderful that we will literally radiate His goodness. Isn't that exactly what we see in the book of Acts? Remember?

Oh yeah, Peter and John had just gone fifteen rounds, sluggin' it out toe to toe, *mano y mano* with the Sanhedrin and finished on their feet like Rocky Balboa against Apollo Creed.

"Hey, Adrian! I *did* it!"

Then, when they're escorted from the ring, the leaders of the Jewish Politburo can only say that "they were amazed, and began to recognize them as having been with Jesus."[2]

What's the difference? Jesus!

157

Think for a moment about what you have in Christ and who you are in Him.

First, Scriptures say that Christ is able to do "Far more abundantly beyond all that we ask or think, according to the power that works within us. To Him be the glory in the *church* and in Christ Jesus to all generations forever and ever. Amen."[3]

Pretty amazing, isn't it?

Simply put, the Christ who lives in us, who chose us in Him before the foundation of the world, is able to do *abundantly beyond* what we can *ask* Him or even *conceive* of in our minds. Why? Because His power works within us! And His glory is manifested within His church!— for all generations. Why? Because as Believers we live in His Kingdom.

Now, if His power is *not* working within you and His glory is *not* manifested in your church, well, the problem is not with Jesus or His word. No, the problem is with you and your church and your impotent Kingdom living. After all, the church is made up of individuals who either live, or *don't* live, in His Kingdom.

And your lack of ketchup stained joy in the simple journey of life will lead others, and yourself, to **Love Jesus** and **Hate Church**.

Next, Scripture says that we have been "bought with a price and that we are no longer our own."[4]

Oh, and what was that price?

It was nothing less than the blood of the Son of God!

Do you know what that means? Simply put, it means you are extremely valuable to Christ. Valuable beyond understanding. You have been chosen by Christ to become part of His family, to live in His Kingdom. You have been inhabited by the very Spirit of God who is "your deposit of the future inheritance to come."[5]

In other words, quit whining and complaining and moaning and lamenting and sniveling and "woe is me-ing" about the little irritants of life, and live like the boy with the big red ketchup comma on his Winnie the Pooh shirt.

Live free from the crud of this world and know that Christ has set you free from the bondage of sin.[6] How? By placing you in His Kingdom— the Kingdom of God.

Wear your stained Pooh shirt as a testimony to the entire human race that you've had a great time with *someone* you love— doing *something* you love to do. "Hey, it doesn't get any better than this!"

Finally, let me run a few positional promises from the Scriptures by you. Just so you'll know exactly who you are in Christ and what living in the Kingdom of God is all about:

I Am Accepted!

- **I am God's Child** – John 1:12
- **I am a friend of Jesus Christ** – John 15:15
- **I have been justified** – Romans 5:1
- **I am united with the Lord** –1 Corinthians 6:17
- **I have been bought with a price and I belong to God** – 1 Corinthians 6:19-20
- **I am a member of Christ's body** – 1 Corinthians 12:27
- **I have been chosen by God and adopted as His child** – Ephesians 1:3-8
- **I have been redeemed and forgiven of all my sins** – Colossians 1:13-14
- **I am complete in Christ** – Colossians 2:2-10
- **I have direct access to the throne through Jesus Christ** – Hebrews 4:14-16

I Am Secure!

- **I am free from condemnation** – Romans 8:1-2
- **I know that God works for my good in all circumstances** – Romans 8:28
- **I am free from any condemnation brought against me and I cannot be separated from the love of God** – Romans 8:31-39
- **I have been established, anointed and sealed by God** – 2 Corinthians 1:21-22
- **I am hidden with Christ in God** – Colossians 3:1-4
- **I know that God will complete the work He started in me** – Philippians 1:6
- **I am a citizen of heaven** – Philippians 3:20
- **I have not been given a spirit of fear** – 2 Timothy 1:7
- **I am born of God and the evil one cannot touch me** – 1 John 5:18

I Am Significant!

- **I am a branch of Jesus Christ, the true vine** – John 15:5
- **I have been chosen and appointed to bear fruit** – John 15:16

- **I am God's temple** – 1 Corinthians 3:16
- **I am a minister of reconciliation for God** – 2 Corinthians 5:17-21
- **I am seated with Jesus Christ in the heavenly realm** – Ephesians 2:6
- **I may approach God with freedom and confidence** – Ephesians 3:12
- **I can do all things through Christ, who strengthens me** –
  Philippians 4:13[7]

Bottom line: If you understand who you are in Christ and what He has already given you— then petty problems that rob you of the *joy* and the *abundant life* He promised will disappear like the morning dew. You'll find yourself blissfully smiling like the little boy with a wad of ketchup on his shirt rather than being overwhelmed by stuff that...well, just happens.

You'll come to understand childlike faith. Childlike trust. Childlike joy.[8]

And you'll begin to forever free yourself from being someone's reason to **Love Jesus** and **Hate Church**.

part three

PLAYING WITH THE PLAYERS THAT DRESS FOR THE GAME

How to make sure we never get into this nasty mess again

people do what they want to do

"Have you found Jesus yet, Gump?"
"I didn't know I was supposed to be looking for him, sir."
From the movie, *Forrest Gump*, 1994

I want to share a couple of truths with you that I have learned from being in the ministry for what seems like a millennium and a half. Maybe that's a bit tongue and cheek. Just my poetic license running amuck again. Ugh.

Actually, it *seems* like I've been in the professional... uh, how would you say— the professional pastorate for most of my adult life. But as far as my time in real, Spirit-empowered, non-wood, hay, and stubble ministry goes— I guess I'm still just a zygote, an embryo, just a middle-aged family man trying to unlearn what the Church system has taught me, and earnestly desiring to learn, first-hand, what following Jesus and living the "abundant life" He promised is all about.[1]

I'm now beginning to see, for the first time in my life, what Jesus meant when He said, "But an hour is coming, and now is, when the true worshipers shall worship the Father in spirit and truth; for such people the Father seeks to be his worshipers."[2]

What keeps *you*, or *me*, or the redeemed church made up of the likes of *you* and *me* from being the type of worshiper that the Father seeks? What could it be? What could be so all-fire important or so blissfully wonderful that we would let it stand in the way of becoming a member of the Worship Minutemen? Oh, you've never heard of these guys? They're the ones who will drop everything at a moment's notice and render to the Lord the worship He desires. They are the faithful ones, the ones He knows He can count on to worship Him in "spirit and truth." Can you imagine? Can you even grasp the indescribable joy of being one of the creations the Creator of All seeks in regards to spirit and truth, true worship?

Wow! It really blows my mind.

The very idea that it's possible for us to be the kind of people He seeks to bring Him unsurpassed glory and honor makes me want to once again ask the probing question, "What keeps His church from being filled with the 'spirit and truth' worshipers the Father seeks?"

Well, I think I may have found *the* answer. Or, at the very least, *an* answer.

And I want to share it with you in the hopes that we will see ourselves and change, or do whatever is necessary to become the "true worshipers of the Father" that Jesus spoke about.

After all, compared to this, everything else in life is pretty much like oatmeal— bland, boring, pale and not very satisfying.

The Two Truths

There are two nagging, undeniable, obvious like a stick-in-the-eye truths about church and ministry that I want to share with you in order to shine some light on the questions asked above. I guess you could call them the sum total of my years in the professional pastorate. If I were to condense, boil down and dehydrate all the experiences I have had over the years with church people, both good and bad, and sift off the common, underlying elements that run through them all, I believe I could summarize church life in the following two broad-brush truths.

Are you ready? Good.

So hang on or sit down, because the first truth is really profound.

Truth Number One:

"People do what they want to do."

I know most of you are probably saying, "Duh? Like tell me something I didn't already know."

Sorry 'bout that. But give me a minute and I think I will.

Now I don't have a particular scripture verse or a single proof text to back up and support **Truth Number One**. But what I do have is a wheelbarrow full of Biblical themes that run the gamut of Scripture, both Old and New Testament, and a boatload of experiences that will convince you that **Truth Number One** is, in fact, *true*. Come to think of it, we'd better make that a *big* boatload of experiences. Maybe even a barge.

Oh, so you want to hear about some of those experiences? You want me to tell you about some of my experiences in church— you know, probably some of the *same* experiences that *you've* had in your church— experiences that clearly affirm the fact that people, no matter what their intentions, are basically going to do what they want to do. Is that what you're looking for?

Ok, try this one on for size.

LaGrange or LaGrunge?

I'll never forget when I was presented the opportunity to pastor my first, full-time church— Emmanuel Baptist Church in LaGrange, Georgia— which is a little mill town located on I-85 between Alabama and Atlanta (that's right on the buckle of the Bible Belt for those of you not familiar with the South).[3] I was so excited about the prospect of being a pastor, *full-time*, that I couldn't think or talk about anything else. God had finally answered my prayers and was going to use me to pastor one of His churches. (Yeah, slap, slap, slap, high-fives all around). I was awed by the blessing God had given me.

After all, this was my solo shot. My maiden voyage. It was my first time to lead a group of people to the promised land of spiritual intimacy and Christ-pleasing ministry. It was so thrilling to dream about uniting, arm in arm, in partnership with a committed, vibrant, fired-up congregation of Spirit-filled Believers that were just as passionate and focused about seeing LaGrange won to the Lord as I was.

Yeah, right.

For those of you who have never had the privilege of serving on a Pastor Search Committee, or Pulpit Search Committee as it is sometimes called, let me give you a quick tutorial. Basically, the entire procedure plays out like a primitive mating dance between the pastor and the church, where the pastor dates the congregation and the congregation tries to woo the pastor.

More often than not, it goes something like this.

The Pulpit Committee is primarily made up of a group of leaders, family heads or spiritually-minded people (hopefully?) who have either been elected or appointed or shanghaied or drafted at gunpoint by the congregation at large to serve as their "search and acquire" agents. They have a mandate from the congregation to fill the pastor spot and complete the church leadership roster— or to put a name in the empty slot on the sign outside that says:

Emmanuel Baptist Church
Pastor _____

Their primary job, or so it would seem, is to either tell you what *they* think you want to hear about the church's direction and goals and vision and history, or tell you what *they* think the church really wants in regards to a pastor.

It's a sales job either way you look at it. Smoke and mirrors.

Afterwards, when your first anniversary as the pastor of the church has come and gone, you sit back and scratch your head and wonder how a group of people duly elected to fulfill the desires of the congregation could have misread them that badly.

"I mean, how could they have been that far off? We're talking about miles off. Light years! It's like the church they described to me and the church I now pastor come from different planets. In different universes!"

Sometimes, it almost borders on criminal fraud.

Anyway, back to the mating dance.

You tell them about you and they tell you about them. Everyone is all smiles and on their best behavior.

But for some reason, things at Emmanuel just didn't seem quite right. It wasn't anything that I could put my finger on. It was more like a feeling, an intuition. I felt like the committee wasn't always telling me the whole truth— like they were purposely leaving out some details. And it seemed to me that I felt this way just about every time they opened their mouth!

"We're looking for a pastor who will help us grow deeper in the Lord."

"We want to move out. We don't want to be inward focused."

"We are looking for God's man to do something here in our midst."

"We want to win our community for Christ."

Looking back, these people must have been on crack.

So you sit down with your family, commit the ministry opportunity to fervent, expectant prayer and spend countless hours daydreaming about how fabulous it's going to be to live and minister around a bunch of Believers who are as sold-out to Jesus as the ones at Emmanuel seemed to be.

What paradise!

What utter bliss!

It surely can't get much better than this!

"Why am I so blessed?" you ask the Lord with genuine joy in your heart and this stupid, naive, slaphappy grin on your face. "Lord, why me? Why did you choose me?"

Then less than two years later— uh, make that two long, arduous, disappointing years on the religious Trail of Tears, you're still asking the Lord the same questions. Only this time the smile and the joy are gone.

"Lord, with all the millions of people in the world You could've sent to Emmanuel Baptist Church... why me? Why did You choose me? What did I ever do to You?"

So we packed the house, loaded up the kids and moved to LaGrange.

We were beaming, slam full of anticipation and confidence that God was going to do something wonderful in this church. Something beyond anything we could even imagine or dream of.

Problem was, Emmanuel Baptist Church reached its spiritual zenith several years after the Great Depression. From that point on it was straight downhill— on roller blades! Year after year they had struggled for life, coughing and wheezing with the death rattle of a church that had long ago lost its focus and forsaken its first love. Emmanuel was in the final stage of church death and nobody, including the proverbial "Unsinkable Molly Brown" young, new pastor, wanted to admit it or recognize the undeniable tell-tale symptoms.

At first, that is.

But after a while the symptoms became impossible to ignore.

It was like trying *not* to notice the clinging stench of a decaying corpse rotting in the middle of your dining room. No matter how hard you try to convince yourself that "you know, the smell's not really all that bad" or how hard you try to fill each day with the busy activities of life in the vain hope that maybe the smell will go away or maybe you just won't notice it any longer— at some point in time you simply must face the stinking reality that you're living in the midst of something dead.

And there's nothing you can do to change that.

"What did you learn?" you may ask like Yoda to young Skywalker. Many things. Some good and some not so good.

But one of the first things that was permanently imprinted in my brain is the simple fact that people— young and old, male and female, rich or poor, Christian and non-Christian— do what they want to do. **Truth Number One**. They're the master of their own fate and will go down swinging just to keep it that way. Hey, if it feels good to them, is deemed profitable or somehow benefits them personally, financially or even adds to their inner sense of well-being, self-worth or intrinsic importance— count them in!

They'll "climb every mountain and ford every stream" to make whatever sacrifice is necessary or required to accomplish what they put their hands to. What they want to do. What's important to them.

Why?

People Do What They Want To Do!

Because people do what they want to do! Always have and always will. And if you recognize the validity of **Truth Number One**, then you must also realize that the opposite of **Truth Number One** is also true.

People *won't* do what they don't want to do. I'll simply call that **Truth Number One (a).**

Come on, think about it.

If people do what they want to do, then it stands to reason that people *aren't* going to do what they don't want to do. They're just not. Why? Because change is hard— and painful. And we don't like pain. The fact is that no matter how hard you nag them or encourage them or implore them or even try to shame them— people *aren't* going to do what they don't want to do.

As the doorkeeper said to Dorothy in the Wizard of Oz, "Ain't no way. Ain't no how!"

Want proof?

Ok, pick any Sunday after church and follow the caravan of minivans to the local All-You-Can-Eat feeding trough. Stroll up to the first group of overweight Baptists you see and say, "You know, the fried chicken isn't really healthy, why don't you try the salad bar instead?" Or, "You're going to ruin your diet if you eat that. Be strong. Stay focused. Just say, *no*." Or, "Look Bertha, you can barely squeeze into those pantyhose as it is now. Just think what that dessert is going to do to you. Material can only stretch so far.

If you eat that dessert you'll be busting out all over and all of us will lose our appetite!"

Three days later when you finally come-to and pick yourself up off the restaurant floor, remember **Truth Number One**— people do what they want to do. And **Truth Number One (a)**— people won't do what they don't want to do. No matter how many facts you throw at them or how well-meaning your words of encouragement are.

It just ain't gonna happen.

It's like trying to lead a dead dog on a leash. He's not going anywhere. The best you can hope for is to drag him around behind you and try to convince your friends and neighbors that are giving you these strange, puzzled stares that you're really just taking him out for a walk. Both of you having a good time. Walking together.

"He's just tired, that's all."

Nope. Hard sell.

It's just not going to happen.

People Do What They Want To Do

Now, I could give you example after example of specific, personal situations where Believers, when faced with a choice of doing what is right, Christ-exalting and Spirit-minded, will almost *always* choose the path of self-gratification and blindly follow what feels good for the moment or "seems right in our own minds."[4]

It's the same dilemma Paul spoke about in his letter to the church at Galatia when he wrote, "But I say, walk by the Spirit, and you will not carry out the desires of the flesh."[5]

Yeah, I could give you numerous personal examples to prove the point.

But I won't.

Instead, let's look at a few of the big guys and see if they practiced **Truth Number One**.

Abraham could have told the truth about Sarah being his wife when he fled to Egypt from the land God had given him to escape the famine. He could have honored and protected her and been an example of a Godly husband and provider to his kid (who later did the same thing to his own wife. Like, duh!). He could have placed his trust in the Lord and not in the fear of man. He could have thought more about the ones he loved than he did about himself.

169

In other words, Abraham could have walked by the Spirit and not given in to the desires of the flesh.

He *could* have. He *should* have.

But he didn't.

Moses could have continued in the path of humility and spiritual intimacy with God and joined the other desert travelers as they set up camp in the Promised Land. He could have followed God in earnest and retained an almost unparalleled, face-to-face relationship with the Creator of All. He could have spoken as commanded and not struck the rock with his staff to bring water gushing to the grumbling, never-satisfied, chronically complaining, redeemed children of Israel. He could have also never uttered the thoughtless words, probably uttered in sheer frustration, "Shall *we* bring water from the rock" and, in doing so, pridefully deflected God's glory from the Creator to himself.[6] (I can imagine God saying, "We? Tell me Moses, what was *your* part in bringing water from the rock? What was your part in the 'we' of this?")

In other words, Moses could have walked by the Spirit and not given in to the desires of the flesh.

So much Moses *could* have done. So much he *should* have done.

But he didn't.

David could have been out leading his armies during the time of war instead of just hanging around the palace, bored, twiddling his thumbs, with *way* too much time on his hands. He could have shielded his eyes or looked the other way when, by chance, he saw a woman who was married to one of his friends bathing alone on the rooftop. He could have said "no" to his lustful thoughts and sexual fantasies and not bloodied his hands with the stain of adultery, deceit, and murder just to have her fulfill them. David, a "man after God's own heart"[7] could have spared himself the horrid judgment of God that was delivered by the prophet Nathan as he proclaimed the chilling words, his bony finger pointed, aimed directly at the center of David's chest, "You are the man!"[8] David could have even experienced the incredible joy of seeing his son grow into manhood and taking a wife for himself— of seeing his son raise his own children. David could have even held in his own arms the grandchildren, maybe *many* grandchildren, that would have filled his aging heart with such peace and purpose as his hair grayed and his steps slowed with the passing of years. Instead, David had to relive, over and over again in living color on the anniversary of the innocent child's death, the sad, guilt-ridden memory and pain of the consequences of his own sin.

170

Oh, the sleepless nights David could have been spared had he walked by the Spirit and not given in to the desires of the flesh.

So many things David *could* have done. So many thing that he *should* have done.

But he didn't.

Elijah could have finished the task God had given him strong— out front and on top. He could have retired the Undefeated Heavyweight Champion of the world. Think about it, Elijah, the one with the Rocky, "I'm not going down no more" spirit, boldly stood and single-handedly stared down 450 prophets of Baal on Mt. Carmel. That's 450 to one! Not great odds in our way of thinking but chump change for the Lord. Elijah could have then faced Jezebel with the same quiet, unnerving confidence and determination like Gary Cooper in "High Noon" and not run, tail between his legs, praying to die, totally panicked, like the lovable poster boy of worrisome wimpiness, Barney Fife.

In other words, Elijah could have walked by the Spirit and not given in to the desires of the flesh.

So much Elijah *could* have done. So much he *should* have done.

But he didn't.

The disciples, the twelve, the chosen ones could have determined to honor Jesus during His last Passover with them and not picked and bickered among themselves as to the supposed upcoming pecking order they would be in after the Great Judgment. Can you imagine? Jesus had just told the twelve how much He "earnestly desired to celebrate this last meal with you before I suffer."[9] He had lovingly washed their feet in order to show them what true humility, true ministry, and real life in His kingdom was all about. The bread, just like His body several hours later, was broken for them. The wine, rich, dark and crimson, was freely poured out for them like His blood would be by noon of the next day. Such humility. Such love.

And the disciples? Grumbling in small groups, oblivious to the intimacy of the moment, more concerned about who would be the greatest in His Kingdom.

Even now, before He was to suffer, Jesus was thinking of them.

And even now, before His death at the hands of violent men, the disciples were thinking about the same thing. They were thinking only about themselves!

Want to know why?

People Do What They Want To Do

Because people do what they want to do.

Truth Number One is true of the members of Emmanuel Baptist Church and equally true about their former pastor— *me*. And I would bet it's also true about *you*.

And your friends.

And your family.

And probably the people you go to church with, and minister along side, and look up to for leadership or look down at in derision.

I'll bet **Truth Number One** is true of your pastor and probably also true of our larger-than-life religious icons and heroes like Billy Graham or D.L. Moody or Martin Luther. Why? Because "doing what we want to do" is our right, or so we seem to think. It's the inbred, hereditary, ever-present curse of our Laodicean, hot and cold, "vomit you out of My mouth" spiritual climate that we live in and have been raised in and nurtured in.[10]

It's pretty much all we know. All we've ever known.

And unless something radically changes, it's probably all we'll ever know.

It has become, over time, the acceptable, *normal* Christian life. The steady, systematic lowering of the bar of spiritual fervency. The slow dimming of the light until we live in the shadowy, gray areas of spiritual apathy and lukewarmness.

Living in the land of Laodicea.

Sad, isn't it?

What I discovered in my first pastorate is that the verbal desires that roll off people's lips, many well-meaning desires and longings may I add, are not necessarily the desires of their hearts. And if the heart says *no*— nothing happens. Why?

Because talk is cheap. Wal-Mart cheap.

We talk about wanting our church to grow…er…just as long as nothing changes.

"Yep Pastor, we want our church to grow. After all, that's why we hired you— to bring in the new people. But that's just as long as the new people understand that Emmanuel is *our* church. Not theirs. We were here first. We don't want any new programs. We don't want to spend any money. And we don't want the music to change one bit. We kinda like the old hymns. Oh, and the order of service has worked fine for us since we came home from WWII so we don't see any need in messin' with that either. And don't expect us to get any more involved than we are right now. You just keep doing what we've always done and things will go fine. Got that? Good. So you go out and win this town for Christ."

In other words, we want growth without change.

Growth without sacrifice.

Growth without commitment.

Give me a break.

Or, as Forrest Gump would say, "Stupid *is* as stupid *does*."

But I also find this true in my own spiritual life. How about yours?

We constantly moan and lament and cry and complain and beat ourselves up over the fact that we're not as close to the Lord as we want to be — yet nothing ever changes.

"I know I need to read my Bible more, but..."

"I wish I had a deeper prayer life, but..."

"I wish I was used by God to win more people to him, but..."

"I wish I had a deeper intimacy with the Spirit, but..."

"I hate the fact that I worry and I doubt and have fears all the time. I wish I had that peace that passes all understanding that Jesus talked about..."

"I wish, I wish, I wish..."

But it's more that just empty wishing.

You can't simply click the heels of your ruby slippers together and mumble under your breath, "There's no place like home. There's no place like home." Or, "I wish things were different. I wish I were more like Christ. I wish my church was better" and expect instant results. Get the point? There has to be a proactive, concrete commitment and sacrifice for things to be different tomorrow than they are today.

Or yesterday, for that matter.

And therein lies the problem. The dilemma.

The church paradox.

Which brings us face to face with **Truth Number Two**. "*If* things are going to change, then I've got to change." No easy way out. No shortcuts. No spiritual pill we can take at night and wake up the next day 20 pounds lighter and 12 years younger.

Nope. "Ain't gonna work that way."

Why? Remember **Truth Number One**.

Because people are going to do what they want to do.

And if things are going to change, then I've got to change. **Truth Number Two**. I can't keep using the same bait and expect to catch different fish.

Really? Oh, yeah.

If I want the outcome to change, I've got to change my bait, the time of day I go fishing, the fishing hole I fish in, the…"

Doesn't that make sense? Nuthin' truly profound 'bout **Truth Number Two**!

Let me drive it all home this way.

Final Exam

Ok. Final exam. Just a couple of quick questions that you've heard before.

Do *you* believe the church can change society?

Do *you* believe the grace of God is stronger than anything Satan can throw at us?

Do *you* believe the power of God is stronger than your apathy? How about stronger than my apathy or the apathy of others?

Do *you* want to be different? Really different? Or, do you want to keep doing the same lifeless, boring, rote religious stuff over and over again that didn't work in the first place and then lie to yourselves by saying that it amounts to something important? Something spiritual?

Do *you* want to experience the *abundant life* Jesus promised us? Or, are you sadly satisfied with the status quo?

Do *you* **Love Jesus**, yet find yourself loathing and **Hating Church**?

If your answer to these questions is yes— then I've got some good news for you! You can change. You can be different.

Take a deep breath and turn the page.

latex gloves
and hands-on ministry

If the **Well-Oiled Machine** were to sing a song to Jesus it
would probably sound something like this:

"I want You. I need You.
But there ain't no way I'm ever gonna love You.
But don't be sad.
'Cause two out of three ain't bad."
Meatloaf, 1977, *Bat Out of Hell*

Our Bathroom Break

This short chapter is what we call our long-overdue bathroom break.
"What's a bathroom break?" you ask.

Simply put, a bathroom break is a small, easy-to-read chapter that's
designed to drive home a key **Love Jesus, Hate Church** point in a single
sitting— long before your legs fall asleep and go numb (if you know what I
mean).

So grab a seat and let's see if we can flush out some **Love Jesus, Hate
Church** truth from the life of Jesus and hold it up and compare it to the life
of the church today.

Should be quite an eye-opening experience.

Latex Gloves and Hands-on Ministry

Throughout the earthly ministry of Jesus we find Him meeting the needs of people in ways that don't seem to make much sense today— in ways that aren't politically correct, esteemed, encouraged, modeled, or even taught by the modern church. How? Jesus met the needs of hurting people with His own two hands.

Oh yuck!

Oh yeah. Jesus had this nasty habit of touching the people He ministered to. Not in the aloof and detached, *Reach Out and Touch Somebody,* Southern Bell kind of way. No, Jesus literally touched people with His own hands. Flesh to flesh.

He was an active participant in the lives of those He changed.

Did you ever wonder why?

He refused to insulate Himself from those the world had forgotten, the discards of society— the throwaways. Jesus intimately involved Himself in the lives of those to whom He ministered.

How different from the church today.

Puzzled? Well, think about it for a moment.

Puss-Oozing Sores: The first miracle recorded in Matthew has Jesus healing a man with leprosy with a human touch. Matthew clearly records that Jesus "stretched out His hand and touched him."[1]

Why? I mean, what's the purpose or point of that? Why didn't Jesus just say the word or think the thought or wave His hand or… anything? Why did He have to heal this man *that* way?

What about the stench of rotting flesh or the risk of contagious infection? What about the opinions of the crowd and the personal scorn and reproach He would bring upon Himself by actually doing something so disgusting, so unsettling and so frowned upon by society?

Couldn't Jesus have healed this man another way?

Answer: Of course.

But He chose not to.

Again, did you ever wonder why?

Maybe Jesus was more concerned about the *whole* man He was about to heal and not just his physical body. Maybe Jesus understood that, from the day the Priest pointed an accusing finger and screamed, "Unclean!"— this man had never felt the embrace of another human. His family, his friends

176

and the church of his day all rejected him as something unworthy of ministry, unworthy of human involvement. Something unclean.

But not Jesus.

Maybe Jesus wanted to give this man the one thing he longed for more than life itself. Maybe Jesus wanted to show him that someone cared— that God still cared. And maybe He wanted to express this love with a simple touch.

Just like the church today, huh?

Yeah, right.

Soured Buttermilk: Later in the same chapter we find Jesus at the bedside of Peter's mother-in-law who was suffering with a fever.[2] What does He do? He ignores the sick, sweet smell— you know, the smell of soured buttermilk that probably filled the room, takes her hand and heals her of her fever.

Why couldn't Jesus have stayed with the rest of the disciples in the living room watching the Atlanta Braves on TBS? Why did He have to go into her room and take her hot, sweaty hand and heal her? Couldn't there have been an easier way?

Let's quickly look at a few more.

Cold Flesh: Jesus touched the lifeless hand of Jarius' daughter as He spoke the words, "Talitha kum!" (which translated means, "Little girl, I say to you, arise!") before giving her back to her grieving parents.[3] Why? Why did He have to take the little girl by the hand? Couldn't He have given her back her life in a way that *we* felt more comfortable with?

Why does Jesus always have to make things so hard?

Dead Eyes: Jesus reached out and touched the eyes of two blind men and instantly restored their sight.[4] See the *whole* scene here— Jesus actually placed His hands on the infected, empty eye sockets of two homeless street people and gave them back their sight. Ugh.

Why? Why did He have to touch their dirty, nasty, crusty eyes?

Couldn't there have been another way to heal these blind men? Maybe a cleaner, safer, more "socially acceptable" way?

Tongue and Spit: Mark records that Jesus put His fingers in the ears and, after spitting, touched the tongue of a deaf-mute man with His spit before healing him.[5]

177

I mean, come on! Isn't that kind of nasty? Extreme? We're talking about overkill here!

Couldn't Jesus have chosen another way to heal this man?

Once again, why does He always seem to make it so hard?

Rubbing Dirty Heads: But Jesus' hands-on involvement wasn't only reserved for the outcasts who needed healing— the health care rejects. The Scriptures also state that He took little children in His hands and blessed them by laying His hands on them.[6]

Why? Because we have this nagging tendency to want to touch, hold, and embrace the things we love, and to keep our hands safely stuffed deep in our pockets around the things we don't— whether they're family, children, friends or blind beggars.

And, like us, Jesus touched the things He loved.

Latex Gloves and Body Condoms

But that doesn't really play too well in the church today, does it?

Nope. Did you ever wonder why?

It seems our current brand of *churchanity* will talk itself blue in the face about being the "hands and feet" of the Lord just as long as we can do so in the comfort and safety of our padded pews. Oh, we can sing a few choruses of the ol' "Here I Am, Send Me…" mission song and preach about it when we begin to feel guilty. But if we're brutally honest with ourselves— that's pretty much as far as the "hands and feet", "walk like Jesus walked", and "I want to be like Jesus" kind of ministry crap goes.

Why? Because we've been taught to minister *only* within the context of the sterile, germ-free, antiseptic environment we've created for our own comfort and ease. We want to bring people to *our* buildings, dress them up in attire acceptable to *us*, teach them the proper etiquette *we* practice and then, "Praise God!" minister to them in the name of the Lord.

Really?

What we end up with is a full-blown case of "do what I say and not what I do" style of ministry.

So what's with the *latex gloves* form of ministry? What's with the attitude that "we want to minister to your needs just as long as we don't get our hands dirty?" Where are those who are willing to touch the lives of others the way Jesus did— without latex gloves or a body condom? Where are those who are more concerned about people than clean carpets, potluck suppers, or choir specials?

How can we sing praise and worship songs to the Father and yet refuse to minister to the least among us He has placed in our midst?

"You know, that's just not *my* ministry." Really? Then what is your ministry?

"I just don't feel comfortable with *those* kind of people." Really? What kind of people do you feel comfortable with? And when did your comfort become the object of what Christ died for?

"God didn't *call* me to get my hands dirty in ministry." Really? What did He call you to do? Did He call you to sit on your fat butt and take up pew space? Is your calling to be entertained on Sundays? Are you called to be a religious Black Hole— you know, to be full of total darkness and sucking up all the light around it?

Is this the purpose God has for your life? Didn't think so.

But it's exactly the kind of ministry that causes people to **Love Jesus** and **Hate Church**.

Makes me sad when I think about it. Does it you?

It should.

Postscript

Our bathroom break is now over.

Now, if you can tell the age of a giant redwood by counting the number of its rings, you should be able to tell how long this bathroom break has taken you by counting yours.

Until next time.

Flush.

is masturbation a sin?

"The church has failed to follow her appointed pathway of
separation, holiness, heavenliness and testimony to an absent
but coming Christ; she has turned aside from that purpose
to the work of civilizing the world, building magnificent
temples, and acquiring earthly power and wealth, and, in this
way, has ceased to follow in the footsteps of Him
who had not where to lay His head."
C.I. Scofield (1843-1921)

Try to think of the most disgusting phrase you could associate with the
present condition of the church. Think of something really nasty. Something
dirty. Got one? Good.

Now try to think of one that's even worse that that!

I bet the one I thought of is *worse* than yours.

Reality Check

"What kind of title is *that* for a Christian book? Masturbation. Ugh!
I'm offended."

Quite frankly, you should be.

But your offense shouldn't be focused on the title of this chapter, on
mere words. No, you should be offended at the truth this question conveys
and how this very question relates to just about everything you've ever done
in church.

Intrigued? Good.

Then let's start by answering the question: **Is Masturbation a Sin?**

Webster Speaks

First, some definitions— just to make sure the words we're using mean the same thing to each of us. You know, to level the playing field somewhat. Common ground type of stuff.

> <u>Masturbation</u>: erotic stimulation especially of one's own genital organs commonly resulting in orgasm and achieved by manual or other bodily contact *exclusive* of sexual intercourse, by instrumental manipulation, occasionally by sexual fantasies, or by various combinations of these agencies.

Sounds disgusting, doesn't it?

If you're like most church-goers, you've probably never heard a sermon on this subject. And if you're a member of the clergy, the ministry, the guy behind the pulpit—

well, you know this subject is strictly hands-off.

Way too hot to handle.

Let me sum up what we know about masturbation. And believe me, I'll try to be as non-offensive as possible.

One, masturbation is a cheap substitute for something God designed for intimacy. Masturbation is nothing more than individual playacting. It attempts to simulate the physical act of love, which God created to be intimately shared with one's spouse for mutual pleasure and procreation, and reduces it to a single, selfish physical event.

Two, masturbation may feel good— but produces no life. In essence, it's a self-gratifying experience that's vain and narcissistic in nature and defies the very purpose it tries to duplicate.

Three, masturbation is designed for the pleasure of only one. That's right, only one— with no concern for anyone else but the short-lived, momentary "good feeling" it produces. It can be like an addictive drug and is the poster child of *self*-centeredness and *self*-gratification.

Finally, masturbation leads to feelings of guilt and shame. Why? Because the very act of masturbation stands as an undeniable proof of the participant's personal failure to have a gratifying relationship with one's own spouse— where the *giving* of pleasure is as important as the *receiving* of pleasure.

Had enough? Ok, then let's take a break and jump into some non-offensive, familiar territory as we begin to answer our question: **Is Masturbation a Sin?**

<u>Note</u>: The following is from the journals of Jacob Simeon.
They were found in an envelope addressed to his children with instructions
they be read after his death.

The Years of Bondage

For as long as we could remember we'd been slaves.

We were born into our slavery. Our parents had been slaves. Our grandparents had been slaves. Being slaves was pretty much all we had ever known and all we ever seemed destined to be.

We were without hope— lost. Helpless to change the certainty of our situation.

One by one, generation after generation, our thin, underfed bodies simply wore out under the load of the Pharaoh's unending building projects, and another desert grave was filled.

No time for mourning.

There was work to do and a schedule to keep and the cruel crack of the lash across a weathered back to make sure the pace didn't slow.

No time to waste. "Time is money!" It was like we were nothing more than disposable parts in a merciless human grind.

Life for our people had been reduced to one continual cycle of despair to death.

And the work droned on, day and night— with no end in sight.

But all that was soon to change.

First, there was a rumor in the wind.

It was said that a man, a strange fellow named Moses, was preaching a message of hope and deliverance. Something about God wanting to deliver His people from the hands of Pharaoh and bring them into a land He promised to their fathers long ago. Something about some powerful signs from God that would force Pharaoh to... oh, how did Moses say it...ah yes, to "Let My people go!"

Nonsense.

As much as we wanted to believe it we just couldn't. We couldn't afford to let our guard down— to take a chance of being hurt again. Why? Well there was work to do and food to gather and families to feed and...

Talk was cheap.

Nothing but empty words.

And empty words don't fill empty bellies.

But somewhere down deep, maybe for only a few of us, a small glimmer of faith was still smoldering. Alive. Waiting to burst into flame.

What if it was true? What if this Moses fellow really *did* talk to God by the burning bush like he said? What if God heard our prayers and really did care about us?

Was it still possible to hope? Was it possible to believe again?

The Countdown

Time quickly proved the truth of Moses' words. The rumor was real.

In a matter of months a series of supernatural events, one right after another, had taken place that convinced even the most cynical among us that God was indeed up to something.

Water turned to blood at the command of Moses. Wow! Scary stuff. Dead fish everywhere! Sure got our attention. We dug new wells and in time everything kind of settled down and got back to normal. Routine.

But not for long.

Soon the land was overrun with frogs and insects. Never seen anything like it in all my life! Everyone sprayed and stomped and cursed and...well, eventually the tide turned against these pests and we finally got the upper hand. Uh, so to speak that is.

Next thing we knew, Bang!— *all* the cattle in Egypt died. Beef prices soared. Over twelve bucks for a Big Mac Value Meal.

Then it seemed like everyone in Egypt caught some sort of disease that caused huge, painful, puss-oozing boils to spring up and fester all over their bodies. The medical community was baffled— totally at a loss as to what to do. Hospitals quickly discovered they were over their head and couldn't handle all the sick. The entire heath care system was on the verge of collapse.

Before the people could recover from the boils disaster struck once again.

For days, golf ball size hail rained down in blinding sheets and destroyed all the crops followed by a plague of locusts like something out of a Stephen King novel. Billions of them, literally blotting out the sun, descended upon the ravaged fields and turned Egypt's prized agriculture into a barren, lifeless wasteland.

Honestly, the grain fields of Egypt looked like pictures of the moon!

And then one morning the morning never came.

Everything remained black as the night slowly stretched on into the day. At first we thought it was a solar eclipse. But by noon of the first day, we *knew*.

Oh yeah, we all *knew*.

The darkness was so thick, so oppressive that you could almost feel it. It clung to you and weighed you down like a wet garment— pulling you deeper into the dark, cold water of your fears.

We all thought it would be night forever.

Panic broke out in many sections of the city. Then chaos.

Martial Law was declared. Curfews enforced.

Everywhere in Egypt, for three long, unforgiving days, the darkness continued.

Well, not *exactly* everywhere.

There was light— day *and* night— in the land in which we lived. In the land of Goshen.

It seemed, just like with the hail and locusts and the cattle, that God spared Goshen and only let His fury rest on the land of Egypt.

Moses kept saying, "Let my people go!"

And Pharaoh kept saying, "Heck no, Mo!"

And more people died and more crops were destroyed and this went on and on and on.

I think it was about this time that God must've grown tired of being ignored.

Moses told us to kill a lamb and paint its blood on the frame to our front door and to stay inside. He said the Death Angel was coming to kill all the firstborn in the land as the final sign to Pharaoh to let God's people go.

So we did as Moses said.

The Death Angel came, just like Moses said.

And I'll never forget that night as long as I live!

Oh, the *screams*...

I can still hear the *screams*— the wailing chorus of thousands of mothers as they discovered the bodies of their dead children tucked neatly into their beds. Try as I may, I simply can't shut out the sound of the cries of anguish from these mothers as they frantically clutched to their breasts the lifeless body of a firstborn son.

I can't imagine their pain or suffering— as we held our own children close, safe, and protected by the blood smeared on our door.

There wasn't one house in all of Egypt that didn't suffer a death that night. Not one! Even Pharaoh's house was visited by the Death Angel.

And that finally got Pharaoh's attention.

The March to the Sea

Things moved rather quickly after that night.

Pharaoh commanded us to "Rise up and follow our God into the desert"— and so we did.

Our neighbors loaded us down with as much of their stuff as they could just to get us, and our God, out of their land. It was like Christmas at Macy's!

"Please," they would plead with panicked, desperate eyes that darted back and forth, looking fearfully for the Death Angel to return or the next calamity to fall. "Please, just take this and *go*. Take whatever you want and *go*. Just please *go*!" People stuffed our arms with gold and clothes and food and... well, we may have been born slaves— but we left like kings!

Moses said God would go before us to lead us into a land "flowing with milk and honey." Can you imagine? Milk and honey! A land of our own! Ah, thank you, Lord!

But there was no time to daydream. No time for sentiments.

Moses, like the trail boss on Rawhide, said it's time to go.

"Head 'em up. Move 'em out!"

And so we did.

There must've been a couple million of us that left Egypt that day. Our procession looked like an army of ants and stretched for miles. Miles I tell you! It seemed to go from horizon to horizon. Lord, it was a sight to behold!

People were singing and dancing. Others were shouting. Most, however, had this stunned, "it ain't quite sunk in yet" or "this has got to be *too* good to be true" kind of look on their faces.

"Is this for real? Are we really free?"

"I can't believe that Pharaoh really let us go."

"Pinch me. This has to be a dream."

"Do you know what a 'land flowing with milk and honey' means?"

And as Moses promised, God delivered.

All during the day God led us with a *huge* cloud. And I mean *huge*! It resembled a stationary, twenty story twister, a category five tornado— but without the rain and damaging wind. It would later become our own DMZ buffer, a Pharaoh-Free Zone, to protect us from the seething anger now boiling in the recently son-less ruler of Egypt.

Anger that was quickly boiling into rage.

Then vengeance.

And finally, revenge.

And at night! Whoa! The cloud turned into a pillar of fire that shot hundreds of feet in the air! It was like God was holding His own torch for us to light the way! Praise Him! I've never seen anything like it then or since!

For days we seemed to wander aimlessly in the desert, traveling in one long, massive concentric circle. Really going nowhere. And apparently not in any particular hurry to get there either. At least that's what it seemed like to me.

God was directing us with fire by night and with the twister by day. But it felt like we were all waiting for something— like *God* was waiting for something to happen. For another chapter to be played out. For the next shoe to fall. For Pharaoh to make another move.

And we didn't have to wait long.

As feared, the heart of Pharaoh remained hard, rock hard— as he mistook our aimless circling for weakness. He convened a quick military counsel, put the troops on high alert and called up the reserves.

It was the time for his revenge. It was now the time for war.

In less than a week Pharaoh was leading the elite First Egyptian Mobilized Armor Division into the desert in a blinding rage to punish and destroy those whose God had punished and destroyed Egypt. They drove on towards the Sea like a madman, like *thousands* of madmen, in a frantic, almost rabid pace— drawing closer by the hour, savoring the kill that was to come. It was as if they could already smell the blood of the Jews, splattered beneath their blades and the spiked wheels of their chariots, as it soaked into the hot desert sand. They were like a Great White, an Egyptian *Jaws*, circling for the final time and rolling up his eyes as he savagely plunged into his prey.

And we— we felt like Quint, trapped and kicking on the sinking deck of the *Orca*.

Suddenly, out of nowhere, Pharaoh and his army appeared as tiny dots spread out across the horizon.

At first we stood in dazed silence, our mouths falling open in disbelief.

Fear and panic quickly followed.

Then misplaced anger.

In a single voice we began to wail and cry and blame Moses for our hopeless situation. We forgot— or maybe we just chose *not* to remember, the plagues in Egypt and how God had delivered us from a life of slavery to bring us to the land promised to our fathers. Or at least, *close* to the land promised to our fathers.

I really don't know what happened to us that day or what we must have been thinking. But we lost all sense of faith— all semblance of reason.

"Is it because there were no graves in Egypt that *you* have taken us away to die in the wilderness?" we screamed, over and over again, until our voices gave out. We had become nothing more than a bloodthirsty mob, reckless, chanting, fever-pitched— demanding that *someone* suffer like we knew we would soon suffer as we watched the dots on the horizon grow larger.

And we all knew who we wanted that *someone* to be.

Looking back, I don't know what came over me or why I so willingly joined my voice with the surging chorus of others. Or why it felt so good, so natural, to shake my fist in anger and defiance in the face of Moses and shout "give us Barabbas."

But I did.

As crazy as it sounds today, I was one of those who screamed at the top of my lungs "it was better to serve the Egyptians than to die in the desert!"

And I stand ashamed and guilty to this day.

On the other hand, Moses stood tall and unfazed, face like flint— a portrait of confidence in his God.

He continued to urge us not to fear. To "stand by and see the salvation of the Lord that He will accomplish for you today!"

But they were just words. Mere words.

And the dots were beginning to take on the shapes of horses, men and chariots.

The Wind from the East

Moses, staff tight in his right hand, stood on a large, Plymouth-looking rock that overlooked the Sea. His arms were outstretched and opened wide, inviting, almost beckoning towards the rough sea. His eyes looked upward, trained on the heavens, steeled, focused, resolute— looking as if he was seeing something kept hidden from the rest of us. Moses stood in obedient anticipation, in confident expectation, much like the pause of a master conductor before launching into the last climactic movement of a classic Mozart symphony.

It seemed that Moses, and Moses *alone*, knew that the best was yet to come.

The rest of us: Brain-dead and clueless!

And then it happened.

The wind began to quietly blow from the east.

Soft at first, gentle, almost like a whisper or the tiny breath of a baby. But soon the wind began to take deep breaths and shout.

And it shouted at us all night long!

God brought the twister and, later that night, the torch of fire to stand between Pharaoh and His complaining, ungrateful children. Moses was unmovable, never lowering his arms or leaving his post. Pharaoh's army never moved from *their* side of the pillar of fire, either.

But something did move.

The water *moved*. And I mean, *moved*!

I'm not sure how to explain what we saw that night. I really don't know how to describe the sound— the screeching, high-pitched howl of the wind and the thunderous rumble of a massive wall of water beginning to pile up on either side of the sea. The sound seemed to resonate in the center of our chest, painful, deafening, reverberating, and echoing off the sides of the canyon wall of water.

It's hard to describe. Almost impossible.

All I can do is just tell you what I saw. "Just the facts, ma'am."

When the dawn finally arrived we found ourselves looking at a mountain pass, maybe the width of a football field, cut clean and dry through the floor of the sea. On either side of the pass the water was parted, stacked upon itself, and rose a half dozen stories into the air. God simply divided the sea for us to pass through to the other side. True to His word, He had provided our escape route.

It was breathtaking— utterly amazing. And it left us stunned with awe.

Moses quickly led us into the pass and moved us to the other side of the sea.

It took all of that day and most of that night for the last of us to make our journey from slavery to freedom. And all the while Pharaoh was pinned down, trapped behind the twister. He was beside himself, growing restless and irate by the minute, fuming, begging his god, Ra, to grant his prayer and let him taste our blood.

As soon as the last of our people made their way up from the dry ocean floor to the safe side of the desert, the twister separating innocent blood from Pharaoh's sword simply disappeared.

Ra, it seemed, had answered Pharaoh's prayer— and off he went!

Like a pack of wild, rabid dogs, Pharaoh's chariots drove themselves down into the mountain pass carved out of the sea like mad, possessed men. They were determined to quickly overtake us and hack us into chunks of bloody memories.

I was standing with my family on the shore of the sea watching the chariots of Egypt charge into the pass that led us to safety. It didn't take long for me to understand what was about to happen.

Sure, we may have crossed the sea in a vain attempt to escape Pharaoh— but we were still helpless, defenseless against the holocaust coming our way.

Nothing had changed. We were still doomed.

Moses' clever slight of hand only delayed the inevitable. Now my children and I would be slaughtered today, on *this* side of the sea, rather than yesterday, on the other side. But the slaughter would take place nonetheless.

And we would all die in the desert.

Naturally we doubted, panicked, and lashed out at Moses.

And naturally Moses stood unfazed by our taunts and confidently encouraged us to "stand back and see the Lord fight for you today!"

The Clean Sweep

What choice did we have?

We simply stood back and waited for what was to come.

Moses, it appeared, heard something from God and stood in front of us with his staff in his hand pointing it like a lance at the line of chariots making their way across the ocean floor at something close to Mach One. As soon as the last of us made it to safety, with no time to spare and Pharaoh's chariots only minutes away, Moses looked up to God and— well, it happened again.

I don't know if it was a tidal wave or a tsunami or something from a movie like *The Poseidon Adventure* or *The Day After Tomorrow*— but in a matter of seconds the walls of water just crumbled down upon the army of Pharaoh.

In a flash, literally, in the blink of an eye— they were gone.

One moment they were driving their teams of horses hard and the next they were crushed by thousands of tons of water. And the sound— *Oh* the sound of *that* much water crashing down and collapsing upon itself was more like something you *felt* rather than heard. It was like standing dangerously close to the engine of a Boeing 747 right before takeoff or maybe being with a NASCAR pit crew at **Lowes Motor Speedway** one Sunday afternoon. It made our heads swim. It was disorienting.

We couldn't even hear ourselves think!

There was one, huge, indescribable **WHOOSH!**— and it was all over.

After only a few minutes the swirling, turbulent sea became somewhat normal and we all began to realize that God had indeed delivered us from the hand of Pharaoh.

Everything He *promised*, He *delivered*.

Some of the children were the first to notice dead bodies and broken debris washing up on the shoreline.

That was all that remained of Pharaoh's army.

Miriam, overcome with what the Lord had done that day, broke into a song.

Soon we were all singing the song.

Would we ever doubt again? *Never*!

Would we trust in the Lord! *Always*!

Well, not really. Wishful thinking.

Our adulation was short-lived— just about as short as our memory.

The Ten Complaints

I'm so ashamed of our actions— no, of *my* actions over the months that followed that I won't honor them by giving you much detail. Oh, I'm sure you've already heard about them. Everybody has. And you well know what they cost us.

Suffice it to say, we refused to be thankful or trusting or obedient from that day forward until today.

First, we told Moses we were thirsty and complained that he had brought us out to die in the wilderness.

Moses prayed and spoke to a rock and the water freely flowed.

Next, we nagged and moaned and whined and complained that we were hungry. "After all," we sniveled, "at least we had *something* to eat back in Egypt. It just *had* to be better than this. Did you bring us out into the desert to die, Moses?"

Again, Moses prayed and every morning God rained down manna for us to eat. And even in this, we were still not satisfied.

"Moses," we whined, "we're *tired* of manna. We're bored. We want something else to eat. We want meat. After all, there was plenty of meat to eat in Egypt."

So Moses sighed and prayed and God flew in clouds of quail. So many we just beat them down with sticks and filled our bellies that night.

And yet, like indulged, spoiled children, we were still ungrateful and still we grumbled.

Again and again we put the Lord to the test.

In fact, God told Moses we had tested Him *ten* times! *Ten!* How? By basically accusing Him of not living up to *our* standards and treating *us* the way *we* demanded to be treated. Every time *we* felt slighted or put out or inconvenienced or annoyed we would arrogantly point an accusing finger and remind the Lord *and* Moses that our lives were far better off in Egypt before the two of them decided to bring us out into a land we had yet to behold with our own eyes. We told them over and over again that we would rather be the slaves of an evil man than the children of a loving God.

What were we thinking! What a reproach to the Lord! We were little more than a bunch of thumb-sucking morons.

Even when Moses was receiving the tablets written with the very finger of the Lord, we were busy creating our own god in the form of an ugly golden calf. A calf! Arrgh!

I can't believe we were *that* stupid.

But we were. And much more so!

One day our disrespect for the Lord rose to a level that demanded a response. It was the one, final blow— our last insult. We'd reached a point where He would tolerate our insolence and contempt no longer.

We decided to take matters into our own hands and sent out 10 spies into the land to check out the Lord's credibility.

"Was it really flowing with milk and honey like He said?" Somehow, we doubted it was.

"Are we able to take the land He claimed to have given to us?" Or, like the brunt of a cruel joke, was it just wishful thinking on His part?

"Do we really want to cross the Jordon and possess the land?" After all, looks like a lot of hard work to me. Maybe we can stay right here and get old and fat.

In other words, we wanted to make sure what He had promised us was really worth having— really worth the effort.

When the reports came back— God was furious. And for good reason.

Think about it, as soon as the spies returned and gave the majority negative report, we immediately assumed the worst about the Lord and jumped feet first on the side of the pundits, the talking heads, and willingly agreed that God had brought us out in the wilderness to die.

"Wow. Some God!" we complained.

Our fervor grew to such a point that we were about to kill Moses *and* the two fools that agreed with him, Joshua and Caleb. We didn't have the ears to hear any good news about God's faithfulness or the fact that, with Him, we were "well able to take possession of the land He promised to our fathers."

No sir. None of us was interested in hearing anything like that.

In fact, we were just about ready to appoint a new leader to take us back to Egypt when the Lord met us at the tent of meeting and the end of all things began.

Let me explain.

God told Moses, "How long will this people spurn Me? How long will they not believe in Me in spite of all the signs I have performed in their midst?" In other words, "How much longer will they trash My honor and My glory? How much longer do they think I will put up with their impertinence?"

Answer: Not much longer.

God informed Moses that enough was enough. We had pushed Him too far.

He decided to destroy all of us as a people and build a new nation on the faithfulness of Moses, Aaron and the two fools.

Thankfully, Moses interceded on our behalf and God chose Plan B.

Plan B

God said, because of our sin, unbelief, and almost criminal disrespect for Him, we would all die in the wilderness and *never* enter into the land promised to our fathers. He deemed us unworthy to receive the gift He wanted to bless His children with.

And, well… He was right.

We were all guilty and didn't deserve anything.

God decreed all those who were *over* the age of 20 would die in the desert because of their sin. Those *under* the age of 20 would live to become seeds for the new nation God would plant in the land He promised across the Jordon.

In essence, God held us accountable for our actions— but showed grace to our children.

It was 38 years ago that God spoke those words to us and divided our nation.

I was 41 at the time. My wife was 40. She died 3 years later.

Think about it, at the very decree of Moses, Israel became a divided nation and her children fell into one of two very different camps.

Camp One: Consisted of all those, like my children, who were *under* the age of 20 when God's decree was given. For each of them, life and worship was to be colored by the hope and expectation of the future fulfillment of God's promise. They greeted the light of each new dawn with a smile on their face and childlike wonder. "Today, *maybe* today, will be the day God will bring us into our inheritance. I sure hope so!"

For them, everything looked up and pointed to the future— to life. Each day was like Christmas Eve. They were the kind of joyous people that knew the *best* was yet to come!

And their life and worship was filtered through that joy.

We, on the other hand, saw things completely different.

Camp Two: Consisted of those like myself and my wife and the million or so of us who were *over* the age of 20 when God spoke those chilling and unforgettable words to Moses. From that day forward, all we could look forward to was death.

Our life had been set— and it was dark and bleak. Our future held nothing but the grave. We would *never* be allowed to enter into the blessed land God had provided for us. We would *never* be partakers of the inheritance. We would *never* experience the joy of hope and confident expectation.

Never.
We were cut off. Disenfranchised.
And we had no one to blame but ourselves.

We greeted each new day with dread— hoping and praying that today *wasn't* the day God would fulfill His promise to His children. Why? Well, in order for the promise to be fulfilled, those under the curse would have to die and our bleached bones litter the desert landscape.

Knowing that, we simply woke up each morning and passionlessly droned on with the routines of life: work, family, church, expecting nothing and receiving nothing.

We were like condemned prisoners— just marking time.
All we looked forward to was death.

Oh, by the way, do you know what we call that kind of spiritual life?
Masturbation. Spiritual masturbation.

Spiritual Masturbation

"Now hold on. What's the point of all this?"
Much! In fact, just like the doomed wanderers in the wilderness, most of what we do every Sunday can be defined as spiritual, religious masturbation.
"Really?"
Absolutely. When we come together on Sunday morning, week after week, year after year, and do the same religious stuff by rote that makes us feel good— you know, the singing, listening to a gifted speaker tell us something in an entertaining manner that we already agree with or that affirms our worth as a person, getting dressed up and going through the culturally acceptable actions for a Sunday, like going out to eat afterwards or visiting with our friends and having a generally good, family-friendly time— but if there is no fruit or life produced by our worship or our gift of service to the Sovereign Lord that created us, then what we do on Sunday, and for the most part, the rest of the week, is akin to masturbation.

Think about it— We go through the motions.
And it feels good.
But it produces no life.
We're just shootin' spiritual blanks.

It's like those who died in the wilderness— faithfully worshiping on the Sabbath but not connecting with the Lord. Being faithful in routine but faithless in heart.

Going through the motions— but expecting nothing but death to come from it.

As Jesus said, "Rightly did Isaiah prophesy of you hypocrites, as it is written: 'This people honor me with their lips, but their heart is far away from me.'"[1]

Please understand, it really doesn't matter where you go on Sunday to masturbate. Whether you're at Bethlehem Community Church where the music is contemporary and the service is informal. Or whether you stop over at First Baptist, which is more prestigious and traditional. Or maybe to First Assembly which is a bit more emotional, somewhat edgy.

Hey, choose your location. It doesn't matter.

The issue is not about where you go to church but about what you do when you get there. The point is, if you and I don't personally change and take the Joshua commitment as a fully committed follower of the Lord, then wherever we attend on Sunday we're just going to go through the motions once again that produce no life.[2]

We'll be spiritually impotent.

Shooting blanks.

The Promise

On the other hand, if you and I individually vow to make a total, life-changing commitment to be forged like Christ irrespective of what the crowd says or regardless of the fact that we may have to stand together alone— and if our solemn desire is to love Him for all He is, above all else, and to let Him call the shots in our life about everything— then Christ will build His church, that's you and me, His *called-out ones*, and has promised He would do some marvelous things through those who follow Him with reckless abandon.

Acts 2 types of things!

And that really gets me excited!

Do you want to be that kind of fanatic for Jesus?

I sure hope so.

Because God is looking for a few good followers.

who you gonna call?
churchbusters!

"What we've got here is failure to communicate."
Strother Martin from the 1967 movie, *Cool Hand Luke*

"We're mad as hell and not going to take it anymore!"
Peter Finch from the 1976 movie, *Network*

Churchbusters. Strange name, isn't it?

In our church culture today— in the church setting we've all grown up in, feel comfortable with, and diligently yet blindly serve— the need for a vigilante, committed, grass roots, missionary, vibrant, radical, church-buster, God-squad in each of our varied cities is of vital importance.

"Really?" you may think. "Doesn't that sound kinda radical?"

Sure hope so.

But by the time you've reached this section of this book, you've probably realized that I am fiercely radical in regards to what is right and just, and I do have a tendency to put forth some... well, how would you say... uh, strange, different, and somewhat unconventional solutions to the systemic **Love Jesus**, **Hate Church** cesspool we're slowly drowning in. Please understand that I make no apologies for my radical stance or my black-and-white way of viewing the things of God. I see it, quite honestly, as the ministry entrusted to me by the Lord.

197

This is just one of those radical ideas that will hopefully spur you on to some deeper thinking and serious soul searching about the "thing we call church" and our co-dependent relationship with it.

Let me give you the background for "church busters".

Peril in Paradise

All across America, in our vested, lukewarm church culture, there are literally tens of thousands of churches that are land-locked.

Well, maybe "land-locked" isn't totally accurate. It doesn't seem like the right phrase.

It would probably be more accurate to say they're *Holy Spirit*-locked.

Yeah, that's it. More descriptive.

Holy Spirit-locked.

These *Holy Spirit*-locked churches that dot our landscape are nothing more than spiritually boarded-up centers of supposed worship and ministry with a **No Trespassing** sign posted firmly on the front lawn.

And there are thousands of them— maybe even tens of thousands.

I'm sure you've seen them all over the town in which you live. In fact, if you live in a town like the one I live in, you can't drive over five miles without running into a dozen or so of them.

"How do you recognize these churches?" you ask.

Simple. You recognize them by their conspicuous *lack* of fruit.

Because of the absence of the Holy Spirit, these are the churches that are *never* going to grow in number, significant ministry or spiritual depth. They're the churches that are *never* going to be innovative in regards to their mission, their vision or their passion. They're the churches that will *never* fulfill the Great Commission Jesus gave them, even if they could remember what that commission was. And, quite honestly, they're the churches that are *never* going to stand aside and allow the Holy Spirit freedom to move among them in His profound, hand raising, "give God the glory" sort of way.

Did you ever wonder why?

Did you ever wonder why these churches never achieve anything remotely close to what God designed and equipped them for?

Did you ever wonder why they're even there— taking up space and draining resources?

Did you ever ask yourself what the people in those churches must be thinking? Or, if they are even thinking at all?

I have. And the answer is both sobering and eye opening.

My Four, No More, Shut the Door

In each of these pitifully sad excuses for a New Testament church there always seems to be a group of people, a family, or a ruling body, that has taken upon themselves the self-proclaimed, prophetic mantel of being the resident church *gatekeeper*.

Every church has to have one.

It's in the Bible.

And if you don't think that it is, just go and ask one of them and they'll be more than happy to set you straight. Pronto.

The single purpose of a *gatekeeper*, the very reason they get out of bed each morning to mess up a new day, is their driving, all-consuming passion to keep the Holy Spirit out of their church and their traditions in.

They're the keepers of the glorious past.

The sentries of the status quo.

The nagging, non-change element.

Gatekeepers have this uncanny ability to manifest themselves into all sorts of different shapes and sizes. They can be young or old, male or female, retired or employed, well educated or dumber than a brick. Their ranks draw from all segments of church society. They're incredibly gifted at being able to conform to their surroundings, much like the way a chameleon is able to change its color at will in order to blend in and remain hidden, unnoticed to the naked eye.

So it is with the *gatekeepers*.

These *gatekeepers* may be deacons or elders or former pastors, or they can take on a variety of hybrid forms and personalities. But more often than not, they usually tend to manifest themselves in the fertile soil of a single extended family, or a group of families, that have rooted themselves into a congregation like kudzu and refuse to be deterred.

"Once they're in, heck, you might as well just sell the farm!"

They may be led by a matriarchal family figure or by an old, retired pastor who has a vested interest to see that things stay the same. Whenever a new pastor, youth pastor, or worship leader comes to serve in the church, they're the ones who vehemently hold on to the way things used to be. To the past. It somehow affirms their ministry or their very existence to see that nothing ever changes.

Change is bad, evil and of the devil. Well, it's hard to argue with that.

"No, we're not going to sing those songs here as long as I'm in this church."

"I don't like to stand during the worship songs. My legs get tired."

"Why do we keep projecting the words on the wall? What's wrong with our hymnals?"

"These kids need to be more respectful in church. Why do they keep running around?"

"I'll tell you when I was a young person, I would never dress that way. It's shameful."

"What's wrong with the King James?"

Usually they work behind the scenes. In the shadows. Just under the radar.

They have this well organized, underground network of church members who never attend anymore and haven't since the late sixties. They're the ones who just sit at home and read the weekly church newsletter to see what's going on, complain about what they don't like, gossip about what they would change if they were there, and generally moan about the current state of things— especially when compared to the wondrous times of constant revival they experienced week after week when they were at the helm, back in their heyday, in the good 'ol days. You know, before the new guys showed up and everything began to change.

Ah, the limitless resources of the *gatekeepers*.

When do you see these people?

Most often at an annual church budget meeting. For some reason the allure and enticement of a church business meeting irresistibly draws them out into the open like a porch light does to fireflies. The pastor stands up to present the budget to the congregation when all of a sudden, instead of the usual 100 or so in attendance, the crowd that Sunday has swelled to 175 or more, 50 of which he's never even seen before. The sanctuary is overflowing, filled to the brim with those obscure people on the church membership role, like the son or grandson that joined when he was 9 years old during a VBS push and has lived like hell ever since. Twenty-six years later he shows up at the annual church business meeting, at his mom's request, to vote with her constituency voting block either *yea* or *nea* on a certain hot, "flavor of the day" political issue. Then, like the homeless, he'll just drift away into the shadows until he is once again called upon to do his family church duty.

Ah, the *gatekeepers*.

"You know, the Pastor makes too much money. He only works two days a week.""We don't need a full-time youth director. We've got too many kids runnin' 'round here anyway."

"What's wrong with the old pipe organ? We've had it for years. Why in the world do they want to go out and buy a new keyboard? Seems like a waste of money to me."

"Hey Pastor, who told you that you can do that, say that, preach that, print that, pray for that, go to that, buy that... ad nauseaum."

Whew! Are you beginning to get the point?

Pastors and other church leaders find themselves habitually frustrated, grossly outmanned, and hopelessly outgunned by the rapid mobilization and deployment capabilities of the *gatekeepers*. And because of the government structures of most churches, they're frankly unable to do anything about it.

When you find yourself continually faced with the "no win" situations described above—

When it doesn't look like things will ever improve—

When yesterday you reached the end of your rope—

And today you find yourself desperately trying to hang on to thin air—

When you've seriously considered resigning from the pastorate to sell used cars—

What do you do?
Where do you go?
Who you gonna call?
ChurchBusters!

"Who You Gonna Call?"

Now, here's an idea, a truly radical solution to all of this.

Suppose in each community there was a group of Believers who were genuinely sold-out to Jesus Christ. Their sole desire, focus, passion, and mission in life was to see Jesus magnified.

That's Jesus.

Just Jesus.

Then let's say this group of committed followers viewed themselves as traveling vigilantes and would move from church to church, as the need arose, in order to restore order and to set things straight. Their ministry would be to weed out the dead wood, to remove the *gatekeepers*, and to let the Holy Spirit flow.

Personal Note: I had this illustrated to me in a rather riveting way several years ago when, upon considering accepting the pastorate of a Baptist church in North Carolina, I had the Director of Missions (that's the local Southern Baptist guy that acts as a paid liaison between the Convention and the local churches) tell me that "the only thing holding that church back from being what God wants it to be could be satisfied with a couple of well-placed funerals."

I'm sure he wasn't actually praying for literal funerals... but I *did* get his point.

He recognized, in other words, that as soon as the *gatekeepers* left, or were removed, or died, or were voted out of power, or the governmental structure of the church somehow changed, the formidable roadblocks and hidden landmines that land-locked the church in spiritual apathy would be gone and God would be able to freely move within the congregation.

Now, I know God can do anything He desires and that "He is in His heavens and does what He pleases."[1] But my experience has been, and probably so has yours, that He is more prone to move in a glorious fashion when His people are focused on Him and His glory— and not on their own petty, self-seeking, inward-focused agendas.

Anyway, the Director of Missions was trying to warn me that God was not likely to move in this particular church under the current setting because the membership deck was stacked with experienced, seasoned, battle-hardened *gatekeepers* who would tirelessly recruit virtual strangers to achieve their pre-determined ends.

"They would," he warned, "spare no expense and leave no stone unturned to accomplish what they want."

These *gatekeepers* would fan out in all directions to shake the bushes, drum-up support, and trade whatever political favors were necessary to ensure a packed house at the next church business meeting. They wanted to flood the pews with "their" people, like-minded zealots, the current and future *gatekeepers*.

Their goal: To stand in mass and shout their opinions and declare as loudly as permissible what they collectively agreed or disagreed with...uh, usually the latter. (The Director of Missions was right. Maybe I should have listened to him.)

That's when you call for the **Churchbusters**.

The pastor, after having experienced a series of set-up shut-downs at the church conference or the annual business meeting, finds himself in the sad and pathetic situation of not knowing what to do or where to turn. Traditional Seminary training is enormously, incalculably deficient in regards to this aspect of ministry life.

Bang! One vote and the Youth Pastor's salary went from full-time to part-time for no apparent reason.

Bang Again! Another show of hands and foreign mission money is slashed in favor of buying a new van to take the seniors out on their "greet and eat" meetings.

What am I going to do?

Who am I going to call?

So, in dire desperation, the pastor picks up the phone and dials:

1-800-CHURCHBUSTERS.

Who Needs a Bible, We've Got a Constitution and By-Laws

The constitution and by-laws, for example, of most Baptist churches were written by the *gatekeepers*. It's true. They were the ones that wanted to make sure that they, or their descendants, always served on all the important, policy dictating committees.

Think about it.

They're the Chairman of your **Finance Committee** placed there to control the money, funding, and direction of the church.

They're the Chairman of the **Personnel Committee** strategically positioned to control the pastor, the staff, their salaries, raises, vacation time, and to write out job evaluations and descriptions.

They're the ones that make up the majority of the membership on the **Youth Committee** to guarantee that their children and grandchildren are first and foremost leaders in the Youth Group.

They're the ones usually in charge of the **Worship Committee** whose purpose is to make sure that, even though the church voted to hire the new "Willow Creek" style worship leader, he still must sing the old hymns from the old, outdated hymnals.

They're also the ones in charge of the **Building and Grounds Committee**. They are there to determine whether the church builds a ball-field as an outreach to attract families within the community or if we install park benches up and down the church property so the members can have a place to sit.

Well, you've met the *gatekeepers*. What do you think? [2]

Been There, Done That

Several years ago I was officiating one of the infamous annual church budget meetings in the very church the Director of Missions warned me not to take. Remember him? Shows you how hard-headed I can be, doesn't it?

Anyway, in this particular church there was a group of people, no... it was more like a *gang* of people, like an al-Qaida sleeper cell... that really had their panties twisted in a wad towards the Youth Pastor and wanted him gone. No mercy. Vamoose. "Outta here, bub."

In late November we had our budget planning committee meeting to formulate the actual budget that was to be presented to the church right after Christmas. The budget planning committee was made up of all the various department heads— finance, stewardship, worship, personnel, building and grounds, and the like. As expected, many of the *gatekeepers* served as department heads and committee chairmen and had done so without interruption since the end of the Vietnam War.

What amazed me then, and still does today when I think about it, is that each of the *gatekeeper* committee heads that were responsible, by virtue of their leadership position, to help formulate the budget simply refused to attend and, in effect, boycotted the planning meeting. This left the remaining committee members in the awkward position of having to create and submit a budget based on their input alone. Why? Because the *gatekeepers* were absent. AWOL. Little did I know they were planning their own December 7th, 1941. They neglected their duty, treated the budget others had prepared in their absence as taboo, vehemently refused to have any input into the process and then began a systematic "rape and burn" campaign against the Youth Pastor in the hopes of building support for a reduction in his salary (he was making less than $8,000 a year as it was) and his ultimate demise.

Wow! And people wonder why we **Love Jesus** and **Hate Church**.

Finally, the anticipated night of the **Annual Church Budget Meeting** came and the budget was presented to the church for passage.

"We have a motion to accept the budget as presented. Do we have a second?"

"Second."

"Is there any discussion on this budget before we place it before the body for a vote?"

Man, what a mess! The best way I could describe it to you is to say that all Hell broke loose on planet earth. You would of thought we were saying Professional Wrestling was fake or something!

Out of nowhere people I had never seen before, the obvious spawns and offspring of the *gatekeepers* who had been kept under wraps until the opportune time, presented themselves, and began to initiate a well-rehearsed slander campaign against the Youth Pastor, saying things that were simply not true. Making irritating innuendoes and blatantly false statements about things and situations they had heard from the *gatekeepers* and had no knowledge of personally.

In fact, the majority of the obscure offspring had never even met the Youth Pastor and couldn't have picked him out of a police lineup if their lives depended on it.

The whole meeting was rapidly digressing into a distressing situation.

As moderator, it was my responsibility to facilitate the meeting and not act as an active participant. I was, to the best of my ability, to remain neutral. Which was getting harder and harder to do.

Edmond Burke's famous quote began playing in my mind:

All that is necessary for evil to flourish is for good men to do nothing

No problem, I thought.

There are plenty of people— good, honest, God-fearing people— who know the truth and won't let this stuff go unchallenged. The good people will do something to stop this evil from flourishing.

Boy, was I naive. Wet behind the ears. Just plain stupid.

I looked around at the other people in the church who supported the Youth Pastor, those I personally knew to be spiritually minded and who were appalled and sickened at what was happening. I looked at each one, eye to eye, waiting, hoping, longing for them to stand and counter the accusations— praying for someone, *anyone*, to have the courage to speak the truth and to stand for what was right.

Did I ever learn a lesson about the powers of the *gatekeepers!*

The "good men" as Edmond Burke would say, "did nothing"— and evil flourished. They just shook their heads in disgust. Disgust veiled as resignation and apathy. A couple of them, leaders in the church, actually got up and left the meeting as some sort of lame protest which did nothing more than further dilute the impact of the spiritual members in that meeting. Somehow they felt they were serving God by doing nothing. What were they thinking?

The budget wasn't passed. It went back to the table.

The Youth Pastor left. Probably the best thing for him.

And I experienced the crowning blow in my graduate level life lesson of how to **Love Jesus** and **Hate Church**. I resigned the following month and have *never* set foot in a traditional church since. Never! And you know what, I haven't missed the stuff at all. In fact, my spiritual life has been blessed by *not* attending. Try to teach that truth in Seminary, why don't ya?

But that's a topic for another time and another chapter.

Pick Up That Phone and Make That Call!

What should I have done?

Simple. I should've called the **ChurchBusters**.

I should've picked up the phone and dialed:

1-800-CHURCHBUSTERS

Or, I could've logged on to their website, **www.ChurchBusters.com** and explained the problem. (Oh yes. There's actually a **ChurchBusters** website. Check it out at **www.ChurchBusters.com**)

My conversation may have gone something like this.

"When is the next church business meeting?"

"Two weeks from this coming Sunday."

"Great. How many do you think you'll need?"

"Well, probably 50 will do. No, let's make it 60 just to be sure."

"OK. See you Sunday morning."

The following Sunday we have sixty visitors show up in our church. That's sixty people who passionately, in word and deed, love the Lord with all their heart. Sixty committed people who are on a quest to see **Church: Jesus Style**— the way He intended it to be. Sixty praying Believers who are following the ministry God called them to without reservation. Sixty people who have a vested interest to root out church *gatekeepers* at any cost. Sixty people who want to see the *church* as a place where Christ is glorified and people are affirmed, strengthened, and encouraged— not a place of pain, deceit, and hurt.

Sixty people who **Love Jesus** and **Hate Church**.

Think of it, sixty new people— husbands, wives, children— all sitting in church.

Many of the members of the church swear that revival has broken out. "I can't believe that all these people are here. It's amazing!"

And at the close of the service, at the invitation, these sixty people come forward and join the church. They become active, participating, *voting* members right on the spot.

Two weeks later there's a business meeting. Who shows up? You got it! The sixty **ChurchBusters**! All of a sudden, in the twinkling of an eye, the *gatekeepers* are out-numbered and it's a brand new ballgame.

The budget's passed.

The Youth Pastor's retained.

The *gatekeepers* are removed from their hereditary leadership positions and vital changes are made that were long overdue. Decades overdue.

Bottom Line: The church moves on in the Spirit of the Lord and becomes, unhindered, what He wants it to be.

Strange idea, don't you think?

Maybe too radical?

Well, if you're one of the "good men" who are doing "nothing"— shame on you!

And if you're one of the *gatekeepers*— why would you be reading a book like this?

Either way, it should show us how people who **Love Jesus** and **Hate Church** got their beginning. Where their genesis really lies.

And why they feel like they do.

blowing snot bubbles

"When someone tells me yet another horror story about
church, I respond, 'Oh, it's even worse than that.
Let me tell you my story.'
I have spent most of my life in recovery from church."
Philip Yancy

One of the most gripping examples in all of Scripture of those who **Love Jesus** and **Hate Church** can be found in the next to the last chapter of the gospel of John. It graphically shows how those who claim to love Jesus— those who've been privy to His teachings, have tasted of His intimacy and have had first-hand, eyewitness experience of His miracles— can respond to Him in two totally different ways.

Like polar opposites.

Head versus heart.

With cautious reservation or with reckless abandon.

And it shows this distinction in unmistakable clarity.

It also reveals to us which of the two paths of worship Jesus honors— literally making His revelation of Himself to us virtually undeniable.

Guaranteed. A sure thing.

Finally, it paints for us a brutally honest picture of the church today and of the choices each of us face. Choices about our spiritual life that we simply can't afford to ignore any longer. Choices this book has dropped on our doorstep, placed in our very lap. Choices that must be dealt with.

Choices about Jesus.

Choices about worship, priorities— and choices about church.

It's a fitting end to our **Love Jesus**, **Hate Church** odyssey.

So hang on, and let's take a look at Peter and John and the woman who blew snot bubbles.

The Time That Is...

Scripture is clear.

Jesus said "But an hour is coming, and now is, when the *true* worshipers shall worship the Father in spirit and truth; for such people the Father *seeks* to be his worshipers."[1]

Or, to repeat His teaching in the language of the New Millennium:

"There is a time, a time which is now upon us, when the true worshipers of God will worship the Father in spirit and in truth. No, we're not talking about the false, hypocritical, self-seeking, passionless, stale and lifeless exercisers of rote religion. But those who choose to worship the Father in the mode He has determined to be pleasing and honoring to Him. In fact, it's this very group of selfless worshipers the Father pursues, actively seeking their worship."

Think about it. Jesus said there are some who claim to follow Him that actually get it right! Wow! They truly worship Him— not according to their own standards and dictates or in a fashion designed to be pleasing to themselves, but they truly worship Him!— His way and for His glory.

They literally lose themselves in Christ. They become hopelessly submerged in the total adoration of the Father.

So who are these people and what makes them so special?

How do they worship? What do they do, if anything, that's different from us?

Why is God so pleased with them that He actively seeks them out?

What do they have that we don't have?

What can we learn from their lives?

More importantly, how can we become the type of person God the Father actively seeks as His worshiper?

And finally, how is this the antidote for the **Love Jesus, Hate Church** cancer?

TGIF

The Passover has passed.

The blood-soaked tears of Jesus have long since dried upon the large, smooth rock near the edge of the garden of Gethsemane leaving tiny, thin, crimson streaks as the only reminder of the night's anguished prayers.

Judas, change in his pocket, has surprised the disciples, and Malchus went home with *both* ears and a story to tell.

The mock trials are over.

Jesus was condemned.

And the twelve are nowhere to be found. Poof! Vanished into thin air. Like a vapor. An early morning mist. As if they had never existed at all.

Dawn of that day finds the Lord nailed to a cross between two thieves, writhing in indescribable agony, at a place commonly known as the Skull.

Hanging there— alone.

Come, Take a Closer Look

Draw near, if you will, and take a closer look at this familiar scene.

Look beyond the tortured, brutalized body of the Lord nailed naked to a Roman cross. Look past His choked, labored gasps for breath. Past the horrid, guttural, gurgling sounds that mark His losing battle against the rising tide of fluid in His lungs.

Look past those that surround Him— watching Him, taunting Him, laughing at Him, deriding Him— and you will see a small group of grief-stricken friends huddled close together. Refusing to move. Refusing to leave. Defiantly unafraid. Much like a faithful dog standing guard over the grave of his deceased master.

They were clinging to Jesus until the very *end*.

Whatever that *end* may be.

They were where they *wanted* to be.

Where they knew they *should* be.

They were with Jesus— their friend, their Lord, their God and their life.

Notice also that Peter, Andrew, James, Matthew and the other disciples are conspicuously missing. Absent. AWOL. Nowhere to be found.

Scattered like dry leaves in the October wind.

When we finally track them down we find each of the disciples slinking into the shadows, trying to find solace in the darkness, far away from the light. They're frantic. Frightened. Tail-between-their-legs petrified. Panic-stricken with mind-numbing dread about how the dramatic cycle of events of the last 24 hours will impact their lives over the next 24 hours.

How sad. How incredibly sad.

Those who had confidently, almost arrogantly, pledged their very lives to Jesus earlier that evening were now running blind, like scared children, afraid of the dark.

"Did you see what they did to Jesus? They'll do the same to me!"

"I've got to look out for *me* now. After all, I've got a family to think about!"

"I didn't sign up for this. This is not how it was supposed to end."

"How can I serve God if I'm dead? Huh? Answer me that question!"

"Run legs! Just keep running! Don't stop and don't look back!"

Notice also at the foot of the cross, as close as the Roman guards will let them, next to the dark, damp, blood-soaked mud where the wooden pole of the cross protrudes out of the dirt, there are several people woven tightly together. They hold each other close, almost clinging to one another, desperate, each somehow trying to find comfort from the oppressive grief they individually share together. They're like terrified kittens that have been abandoned at midnight in the middle of a large field. Shaking with fright. Lost and rejected. Holding on to the single hope that their mother will soon return to rescue them, save them, and lead them back home.

But in the deep sorrow of the long night they know their mother isn't coming. They're all alone— together. All they have is each other.

Together alone.

Look and you'll see the disciple whom Jesus loved, John, trying to warm and comfort as best he could Mary, the mother of Jesus. The same Mary, at the dying request of the Lord, that John takes into his own house and into his own family from that very day until her death some years later.

There were some other women at the cross.

There was the sister of Mary.

There was Mary the wife of Clopas.

And there was a woman of a horrendous, pitied past— Mary Magdalene.

Mary Magdalene

Who was Mary Magdalene?
What was she doing with John and Mary at the foot of the cross?
Why was *she* there?
What had Jesus done for her?

When we first hear of this woman we see her displaying, in an unashamed, extravagant fashion, her love and profound gratitude for the precious gift Jesus had given her. In Luke 8:2, it states that Jesus had previously driven seven demons out of her and had delivered her from the dark dungeon of spiritual bondage to the joy of true freedom.

With a word, a command and a touch— Jesus had liberated Mary Magdalene.

For the first time in forever Mary was free because of Jesus!

And now, at the home of Simon the Pharisee, that forgiven, freed, and delivered Mary comes unannounced and uninvited and falls at the feet of the One who had changed her life.

Look again at the scene as it unfolds before us. And take special note of where it's all taking place.

This is Simon— a Pharisee. A religious "I'm-better-than-you" noble.

This is Simon's house   a place where a woman like Mary would have never been invited and would have never felt welcomed.

And this is Mary— the woman with a stained, tainted past. Refusing to be deterred by the scornful stares and muffled rebukes of the "clean, blessed, and good-looking" people, she brushes past those who are chosen and gathered to hear the Master, and shamelessly bows in worship at the feet of Jesus.

"Ugh! Why… why… this is unthinkable!"

"It's unimaginable."

"Quite an embarrassment, if you ask me."

Mary— the known sinner, the town harlot, the local slut— carefully brought out an alabaster vial of costly perfume she had hidden under her shawl and, not feeling worthy to even look upon the Lord, dropped humbly to her knees behind Him. Weeping from guilt and gratitude, she washed His feet with her tears and kept wiping them dry with her hair.

With her hair!

Her long, beautiful, black hair.

The *only* glory of a woman like Mary.

Breaking the vial, eyes downcast, hands trembling, she began to gently anoint Jesus with her perfume. Slowly. Lovingly. In deep worship. Savoring each second, each moment with Him like it was a priceless jewel. She had to show Him, no matter the costs, the depths of her love for her Lord.

Jesus, compassion beaming from His presence, looked at Mary with His faint, familiar, all-knowing smile. And yet He never uttered a word at her worshipful display of devotion and love. It seemed that Jesus was also savoring the moment.

All she was and *all* she would ever be now belonged to Him— to Jesus.

She didn't care what the others thought.

Not now.

Not anymore.

Never again.

It was clear to see that Jesus was well pleased by her actions.

It was also clear to see that the others in the room were not so pleased by her flagrant display of adoration.

It unnerved them. Made them feel uncomfortable. Almost queasy.

While Mary was lost in the deep worship of the Lord, the others sitting around the table were feeling somewhat uneasy about what they were witnessing. The genuine display of Mary's raw emotion troubled them. Anger was soon to follow.

"After all," they reasoned to themselves, "there are *other* ways…you know…uh, proper and acceptable ways to honor a man like Jesus. But this…well, this is too extreme. It's too strange and unconventional. It's not exactly what we would call proper etiquette, is it? And just who does this woman think she is? Who does she think she is to come barging in here uninvited and intrude on this group of upstanding, religious people like us? We've spent the better part of our lives not living or associating with the likes of Mary the sinner. What right does she think she has to come and disturb this gathering? Who does she think she is anyway?"

With each unanswered question, born out of deep conviction, the anger of the Pharisee and his *proper* guests grew.

"If this man were a prophet, He would know who and what sort of person this woman is who is touching Him," Simon the Pharisee said to himself. "After all, she is a sinner."[2]

But Jesus did know.

Jesus knew *exactly* what kind of woman Mary was. He knew of her past, her pain, and her failed hopes. He knew of the unspeakable hurt she kept locked up and hidden deep within herself, buried beneath a façade of flippant cynicism designed to keep people away, never close, at arm's length, so that no one would ever see. And Jesus also knew of her memories— ah, the plaguing, tormenting memories of a small child, alone in the dark, pleading, crying, begging, and praying for someone to help her as her innocence was betrayed, violated again and again by the groping hands of cruel, abusive men.

Oh yes, Jesus knew *everything* there was to know about Mary.

Everything. Both good and bad.

But Jesus also saw something in Mary of great worth. He saw something worth redeeming. Worth saving.

Jesus saw something in Mary worth dying for.

Jesus saw Mary, not for what she was— a hard, arrogant, bitter woman with a biting, sarcastic tongue— but He saw Mary for what she could be. Jesus saw her potential. He focused on the unlimited promise of her future and not on the multiplied failures of her past.

But there was something more.

Jesus also recognized that somehow Mary intuitively knew who He was and what He had to offer her. Somehow she understood the "big picture." New lives in exchange for old. A new beginning. A fresh start. A changed life. Like being born again.

Jesus saw her hunger, her longing, her need, and her faith.

But He also saw something else.

Her worship!

He experienced Mary's unbridled display of passionate worship designed for an audience of just One.

Just for Jesus.

Knowing Simon's thoughts, Jesus said, "Simon, do you see this woman? I entered your house; you gave Me no water for My feet, but she has wet My feet with her tears and wiped them with her hair. You gave Me no kiss; but she, since the time I came in, has not ceased to kiss My feet. You did not anoint My head with oil, but she anointed My feet with perfume. For this reason I say to you, her sins, which are many, have been forgiven, for she loved much; but he who is forgiven little, loves little." Then He said to her, "Your sins have been forgiven." Those who were reclining at the table with Him began to say to themselves, "Who is this man who even forgives sins?" And He said to the woman, "Your faith has saved you; go in peace."[3]

Go in Peace

"Go in peace," Jesus had told her.

Ah, the healing power of those three small words.

"Go in peace."

And so she did.

Mary left that unforgiving house experiencing something she had only dreamed of, something that always seemed to be just beyond her grasp, just past her outstretched fingertips— just out of reach.

Mary experienced real peace.

True peace.

Redemptive peace.

For the first time in her troubled life Mary was free, clean, and forgiven. The flesh of her soul was no longer hard, rough, and callused by the trials and hurts of this life, but it was now made new, soft, and pink, like the bottom of a newborn baby. The peace that Jesus spoke about now belonged to her. It was His peace. Not the kind of peace the world gives... but His peace.[4] The peace that "passes all understanding."[5]

It was His wonderful gift to her.

No more condemnation and no more shame.

No more seeking from man the approval she had now freely secured from God.

No more loneliness or lack of purpose or hollow despair.

Forgiven! She had been truly forgiven!

The gift Jesus presented to Mary that day is the same gift He also offers to each of us. What she became, we can be. Like Mary, we also can be forgiven, redeemed, cleansed, and set free! The same Spirit of God that lives in her also desires to live inside each of us to comfort, empower, and conform us to the image of God.

Wow!

Does This Sound Like You?

The amazing truth I see in this story is the contrast between Mary's reaction to the gift of Jesus and the reaction most of us, the church crowd, have towards His same gift. Let's face it, the party line, the status quo, the acceptable and popular reaction of the church today towards Mary's childlike example of heart-felt gratefulness is "eye-opening" at best. At worst, it is the vilest, most appalling form of sin and apathy imaginable.

218

Oh, you think that statement is a tad too strong?

Well, ask yourself this question. What have you done with your life to show your gratitude to Jesus for the gift of forgiveness He presented to you?

24/7 – 365

Mary spent the rest of her life dreaming up and inventing new ways to lovingly communicate her gratitude to Jesus for the gift He freely gave her.

The Gift: Something she didn't deserve and certainly couldn't earn herself.

Think about it.

From that day forward, without hesitation or looking back, Mary began to follow Jesus. Like Matthew, James, John, Peter and the others who responded to the direct invitation of Jesus to "Follow Me," Mary devoted herself, 24/7, to Jesus and to Him alone.

Do we?

In Luke 8:3, the Scriptures state that Mary, along with some other women who were also changed by Jesus, were contributing to His support out of their own means— as meager as they may have been. Imagine, beginning with the breaking of the vial to anoint her Lord, Mary began to see that she was "no longer her own, but bought with a price."[6] She knew and fully understood that if she belonged to Jesus, if He was truly her Master and Lord, then it would naturally follow that *everything* she had also belonged to Him. Why? Because she was, as Jesus taught over and over again, simply a pilgrim, a sojourner, someone just passing through. After all, this world was no longer Mary's home anymore than it was her Master's home. She now lived in His kingdom and served Him without reservation. She was full-time and totally focused. Mary had successfully made the transition between the two kingdoms— the kingdom of this world and the Kingdom of God. She left the one and, with arms flung open wide with anticipation, eagerly embraced the other.

Just like us, right?

Back to the Past

Back to the cross.

The disciples, save one, are all gone.

The very men who had boldly pledged their lives to Jesus several hours earlier now fled and hid for the very sake of them. The lips that so confidently proclaimed, "Even if all run away, I will die for you!" had just hours later said, "I don't know the man!"[7]

Courage in the light quickly dissolved into fear in the shadows.

Those who knew the truth, or *should* have known the truth about Jesus, had scattered like leaves in the wind leaving their Lord to face the trial of all humanity alone.

Some friends.

But not all ran.

Mary stood with Jesus. She was there for Him as He had always been there for her. She was at the cross to let her Lord and Master know, if only by her mere presence, that not all were cowards. That someone cared. She was determined to show her love for Him to the very end— no matter what.

No matter what.

Then, when Jesus had breathed His last, in the midst of the darkness that turned the afternoon sky black as ink and the rumors of the Temple veil being torn top to bottom, when all hope was lost and her Lord was truly dead and gone forever— Mary was still there. She was steadfast. She refused to leave. She was loyal and committed, a true friend to the end.

Mary knew her place. And that place was with her fallen Lord.

Even as Jesus' body cooled and His limbs began to stiffen, Mary was ready to cover Him with herself, to somehow try to warm the One who had revealed to her the "true" light that had come into the world.[8]

Just like we would have done if we were there.

Yeah, just like…er…us.

Joseph from Arimathea petitioned Pilate for the body of Jesus. The very one who publicly feigned any interest in Him for fear of the Jews, now stepped into the light and took his stand next to the broken, lifeless body of the Lord. When it seemed little more than a moot point, Joseph finally became bold.

With Pilate's permission, Joseph, Mary, and some of the others prepared Jesus for burial as best they could. The day was quickly coming to a close and the Sabbath was dawning. Their time was running out. A few pockets of spices, the loving, caressing, straightening of His shroud, like a mother tucking her child into bed, and their work was done.

At the urging of the Jews, a huge stone was rolled over the mouth of the tomb to prevent…well…*something* from happening. Nobody knew quite what. The Jews warned Pilate that the disciples were going to steal the body of their dead master. Fat chance! Like scared children lost in the dark, that was the *last* thing on the disciples' minds. They were still firmly camped in the self-preservation mode. You know, the standard "Hey man, I got my own problems to deal with, my own family to think about. I know what happened to Jesus was terrible, but man, what about me? What am I going to do now?"

Jesus was buried. The borrowed tomb secured. Guards posted and the huge stone rolled firmly in place. Seal intact.
"Nothing gonna happen here."

The disciples? They were frightened, terrified, lurking in the shadows, running from their own reflections and praying they wouldn't bump into one another.
And the rest? Those who truly loved the Lord? They would have to wait until dawn of the day after tomorrow, the first day of the week, to properly complete for Jesus what they had only begun in haste.

And the long wait began.
Like time standing still.
Seconds dragging on like hours.
Everything moving in slow motion, as if in a dream.
Like the whole world was underwater.

Dusk to Dawn

Saturday. Dawn to dark.
The Passover was officially over.
Dawn of the next day, while it was still dark, Mary made her way back to the tomb of Jesus.

> Now on the first day of the week Mary Magdalene
> came early to the tomb, while it was still dark, and
> saw the stone already taken away from the tomb.[9]

What!
Emotions, one after another, came pounding like the waves of the sea in the midst of a raging Northeaster.
Shock! Disbelief. Wonder. Fear. Panic.

Suddenly the air seemed thick and hard to breathe.

Mary's mind began to race as she desperately tried to make sense out of what she had just seen. Come on Mary, think! Think! Focus only on the facts. What happened here?

Like pieces of a massive jigsaw puzzle, Mary began to put together what she knew. The facts...

Fact: The stone had been rolled away from the mouth of the tomb. "Must have taken several men to accomplish that. It was a huge stone."

Fact: The body of Jesus was gone. "Someone must've taken the Lord. But, where? And, why?"

Fact: The guards? "Sprawled out on the ground like dead men. Why?"

What happened here?

Mary's first thought, "I've got to tell the others!"

She had to tell Peter and John. Maybe they could tell her where they had taken the Lord. Maybe they knew what happened to the body of Jesus. Maybe they would know what to do.

> And so she ran and came to Simon Peter, and the other disciple whom Jesus loved, and said to them, "They have taken away the Lord out of the tomb, and we do not know where they have laid Him."[10]

Her words seemed to just blubber out, rolling one on top of the other, each mixed with tears and weeping. Her words spilled out like a bullet-point memo, not sure when one sentence ended and the next one began. Hey, it was hard enough to think complete thoughts, let alone speak complete sentences!

Peter and John stood and looked at her with blank stares. They were not quite sure they had understood what she said. Maybe they'd missed something.

Did she say something about Jesus? The tomb? Empty? Can't be!

It was John, with his compassionate, soothing nature that tried to calm her down...

"Now hold on, Mary."

"Slow down, Mary."

"Take a deep breath and tell me again."

"What are you talking about?"

"What are you trying to say?"

"I can't understand you. You're not making any sense."

"Come on, slow down, Mary."

"Take it from the top. Tell me again. What's happened at the tomb?"

Stammering with short, jab-like pants, Mary told them once more.

"They have taken away the Lord out of the tomb, and we do not know where they have laid Him."[11] There was something in her voice. Something in the pleading, longing, searching tone of her voice that seemed to shout at them and say, "Look, I'm not crazy. I saw what I saw! Come with me and see for yourself if you don't believe me!"

So they did.

The non-verbal challenge in Mary's voice, coupled with the unbridled passion in her broken sobs, had said enough. Volumes. Mary really *believed* she saw the tomb empty and the body gone. There was no denying that. Glancing at each other with the "Could it be? Naw!" expression on their faces, Peter and John broke into a sprint as they dashed towards the Garden.

> Peter therefore went forth, and the other disciple, and
> they were going to the tomb.[12]

Running hard, legs cramping, lungs burning— yet drawn by an irresistible anticipation that seemed to compel them forward, the trio ran through small fields, around unlit corners and down dusty paths, until they drew near to the entrance of the tomb. As they got closer to the place where the Lord was buried their speed instinctively increased. John, younger, faster, and sleet of foot pulled noticeably ahead while Peter, losing ground with each sandaled stride, followed close behind.

Then, as if forgotten, like an afterthought— came Mary.

She ran, stumbled, picked herself up and ran again, all the while holding up the hem of her garment scandalously high in a fashion that would have brought upon her the disgusted stares and condemning gossip of the pious, judgmental, I'm-better-than-you women still comfortably sleeping in their beds.

Did she care what they might say? Did she care what they thought of her?

Not on your life!

She was going to where her Lord was! She was going to be with her Master!

She was going to Jesus.

John was the first to reach the open tomb. He stood at the entrance, wide-eyed and mouth open, not sure if he should go in. Not sure of what to do or how to feel. Not really sure of *anything* at the moment. Peter, still several yards behind, finally lumbered past him and barreled into the tomb.

It was just as Mary had said!

The body was gone. The tomb was empty. Nothing left but grave clothes.

The linen wrappings were still in place and the face cloth was neatly rolled up and set aside, all by itself, as if by design. Strange? If someone had stolen His body during the middle of the night, why would they have taken the time to neatly fold up the face cloth? I mean, that didn't make any sense. It was dumb. Stupid.

What's happened here? What's going on?

Almost unnoticed by the pair was the presence of Mary. She was on her knees outside the tomb, as if collapsed by the thought of the One she loved with all her heart, laying somewhere else, moved by strange, unloving hands. The sounds of her anguished, almost inconsolable sobs broke the solemn, early morning quiet. The dust, mixed with her tears and caked on her cheeks, gave her the look of a common laborer after harvest time. She resembled a mourning mother who had just learned that her husband and three small sons had been tragically killed in an early morning accident. Emotions run amuck. She was crying uncontrollably in deep despair.

Blowing snot bubbles.

Blowing Snot Bubbles…?

The rest of this story amazes me. It literally confounds me.

In fact, the more I read it the more I'm convinced that the key to true worship— the key to having Jesus reveal Himself to us in a style straight out of the pages of the book of Acts— the silver bullet, the antidote to **Loving Jesus** and **Hating Church** can be found behind the actions of Mary and the Dynamic Duo. You can clearly see that the intensity and degree of their love for Jesus, in contrast to the intensity and degree of their love for themselves, shapes their different responses to the same events that fateful morning.

Remember, it was earlier that very week that Jesus had told them, "he who loves his life loses it, and he who hates his life in this world shall keep it unto eternal life."[13]

And now, on the morning that forever changed history, the morning of prophetic fulfillment, of blessing and awe, the disciples closest to Jesus failed to even remember, let alone understand, what He had said.

Let's look at the response of the two:

First, Peter and John. You know, the "even if all fall away I will never deny you!" disciples.[14]

> So the disciples went away again to their own homes.[15]

What? Did you catch that? Do you realize what just happened?

Peter and John had just left the vacant tomb with its rolled up face cloth and the guards laying motionless, paralyzed, face up on the ground. They obviously walked past, possibly even stepped over, the weeping, sobbing, inconsolable, blubbering-out-of-grief, Mary. And without so much as a single word of encouragement to her, they parted ways as they headed to the safety of their own homes. Wow! Absolutely unbelievable!

Just like nothing ever happened.

Just like they had a lawn to mow or a call to make or an appointment to keep.

Just like what they had just experienced had no affect on them at all.

Like it was no big deal. Nothing out of the ordinary. All in a day's work.

Classic denial.

Are you amazed at their actions? Are you shocked? Maybe angered?

Does their callous behavior seem to be out of character for Peter and John?

Did you ever wonder why, at the very least, they didn't want to spend some time with each other? You know, maybe to discuss what had happened? Maybe to pray?

Did you ever wonder why they didn't have the same excitement running *from* the tomb as they did running *towards* it? Why they weren't overcome with the urge to tell the world what Mary said was true? That a miracle had taken place and Jesus was alive?

Does it seem odd to you, if not down right cold-hearted, that they chose to close their eyes and plug-up their ears to the sights and sounds of Mary's anguish and grief as they stepped over her and slithered off to relative safety, leaving her to cry alone in the dirt?

Does it bother you that they seemed to be concerned only with themselves?

I mean, what kind of men are these anyway?

Where's their love and compassion?

And to think that Jesus called them His friends! Some friends!

Ah, But the Sovereign Choice of God!

Before I begin to bang on these guys too much, let's understand that there's a spiritual principal at work here. The principle is simple: "What goes around, comes around." Or, to put it in Biblical terms, "Whatsoever a man reaps, so shall he sow."[16] In other words, honor breeds honor, love breeds love and disdain breeds disdain. In fact, Jesus said "everyone who confesses Me before men, I will also confess him before My Father who is in heaven. But whoever denies Me before men, I will also deny him before My Father who is in heaven."[17]

Now it's possible that Peter and John wanted to "sort it out in their minds" before telling the others. Or, as men, maybe they needed to "mentally process the empty tomb scenario and formulate a plausible explanation" before reporting their findings to the other disciples in the annual, upper room, board meeting.

They may have been scared. Frightened. You know, that flat out, "pee-in-their-pants" petrified. Or, maybe they were, how do we say, whacked-out, bewildered, and just not thinking straight. "Uh, I don't know what I could'a been thinking. It was like my brain was stuck in neutral or something. It just wouldn't go nowhere." Possibly they could have been suffering from a mild state of shock. Or whatever! Who knows?

The list could go on and on.

The point is this: The disciples were, by their very actions, far more concerned about their *own* hides than anything or anyone else that day. And because they chose to selfishly skip alone to their own homes, they tragically missed the greatest gift of all. In doing so, they stepped over the grief-stricken body of Mary lying in the dirt in a pool of her own tears with no one left to comfort her.

No one.

But Jesus.

> "But Mary was standing outside the tomb weeping; and so, as she wept, she stooped and looked into the tomb..."[18]

Do you know what she saw?

Two figures. Men dressed in brilliant, dazzling white. One at the head and one at the feet of where Jesus once was. Angels! A heavenly visitation!

One spoke to her, questioned her, and asked her with kindness and compassion in his voice, "Woman, why are you weeping?"

Mary replied, her voice halting, choked with childlike awe and emotion, "Because they have taken away my Lord, and I do not know where they have laid him."[19]

Translation: Jesus is gone. Someone has taken away His body. I don't know where they have put Him but I want to be where He is. I want to be with my Lord. My place is at His side, at His deathbed, to care for His body. I *want*, I *need*, I *long* for nothing but my Lord!

How do you comfort a woman so broken as Mary? How do you soothe the ache in her heart? How do you put back together the broken pieces of her life? How do you erase the pain, rejection, hurt, disappointment, and despair she suffered over the last 36 hours?

How?

Well, you don't.

You simply point her to Jesus.

> When she had said this, she turned around, and beheld
> Jesus standing there, and did not know that it was
> Jesus.[20]

He spoke to her.

Looking back, Mary said she should've recognized His face, if not His voice. However, with puffy eyes swollen from days of sobbing she failed to realize that the answer to her life's longing was standing directly in front of her in the garden by His tomb.

So close, yet so far away.

Jesus. The Light of the World and the Lord of Mary's life.

He spoke softly to her. "Woman, why are you weeping? Whom are you seeking?" Supposing He was the gardener, Mary pleaded with Him to tell her what had happened to her Lord. "Sir, if you have carried Him away, tell me where you have laid Him, and I will take Him away."[21] Tell me! Where is He? I want to be where He is.

The Revelation of a Lifetime

It was then that it happened.

Like the end of a playful game of hide-and-seek, Jesus spoke her name.

"Mary."

Joy indescribable replaced grief untold!

In tears of joy she ran, stumbled, crawled up to Jesus and grabbed hold of Him as she lay before Him, facedown, in thankful worship and adoration. She had lost Him once. She would not lose Him again. Never!

"Mary," Jesus said smiling. His tone was full of deep satisfaction at her unreserved, unashamed display of raw, genuine devotion. "Mary, stop clinging to Me, for I have not yet ascended to the Father. But go to My brethren and say to them, 'I ascend to My Father and your Father, and My God and Your God.'"[22]

And after having to lovingly break from her grasp like a father does his three-year-old daughter when, for love, she doesn't want him to leave for work, Jesus and Mary parted.

With the power, the love, the confidence of fulfilled expectations, and the wonder and awe of first-hand proof of a miracle, Mary made her way back to the disciples.

Her message? Ah, you know...

"I've seen the Lord!"

"I've seen the Lord!"

"It's true. He appeared to me. He's alive! He's living!"

"Oh, I've seen my Lord!"

And Now, the Rest of the Story...

Did you ever wonder why Jesus chose to reveal Himself to Mary and not to Peter and John? Does that seem somewhat strange to you? I mean, would it not seem logical, even prudent, for the Lord to confirm His resurrection to His disciples and not to a woman with a tainted, less-than-stellar past? If credibility was ever going to be an issue— why Mary? And why not Peter and John?

I wonder?

Yet, for some reason known only to Jesus, He chose to reveal Himself to Mary.

Did you ever wonder what *you* would have done in the same situation? If *you* had been at the tomb with Peter and John, would *you* have responded differently than they did? Would *you* have been concerned about Mary? Would *you*, like Mary, have only wanted to be with the fallen body of your Lord? Would *you* have blown snot bubbles with her?

Or, would *you* have been more concerned with your reputation, your social status, your financial and personal responsibilities— your very life? Would *you* have gone underground and stayed secluded until *you* could confidently face your critics and confront their nagging taunts of "Told you so! Should have listened to me? Nanny, nanny boo boo!"

Which would it have been? The Lord or your life.
Which kingdom would your citizenship reside? His? Or yours?

Love Jesus, Hate Church

Mary chose the Lord— and all that He had for her. She didn't care what the others thought or what the future held for her. She clearly had counted the cost and determined that the rest of her life began with the words of her Lord, "Go in peace."[23]

From that moment on, nothing of this world mattered to her.

For Peter and John the situation was quite different. They chose their life— and the safety and security of the familiar. After all, they probably reasoned, "an empty tomb is not something to go around telling everybody about. They might think we're strange. Kinda weird."

Peter and John chose themselves— and the desire to always have it the way it had always been. You know, *me* first. They demanded to be in control of their own lives. They would call the shots. They remained the CEOs.

Mary, on the other hand, wanted nothing but Jesus.

So, to whom did Jesus reveal Himself?

Was it the ones who served Him only when it was convenient? The ones who, when confronted with the fulfillment of Jesus' greatest teaching, turned and ran and kept this wonder to themselves? Was it the ones who, after peering into an empty tomb, callously stepped over the ministry to Mary and went home? To the ones who took His light and hid it under a basket so no one could see?[24] To the traditional, religious, formal, individually determined proponents of man-made devotion to the Lord?

I think not.

No, Jesus revealed Himself to the one who truly worshiped Him. The one who honored Him, pleased Him, and expressed love to Him in a way that showed the inner condition of her heart.

Jesus showed Himself to Mary— the true worshiper of God.

How About You?

Now, for a final thought...

How about you?

Has Jesus revealed Himself to you like He did to the Believers in the pages of the book of Acts? Has He spoken to you, ministered to you, called and compelled you to Himself?

No? Not sure? Really?

Ever wonder why?

Could it be that, like Peter and John, you're so concerned with appearances and how this life of Christ will affect you that you failed to worship Him in a fashion pleasing to Him? Mary wasn't the least bit concerned with what others thought about her devotion to her Lord.

Are you?

When you gather together to worship are you internally constrained by the perceived reaction of those who surround you in church? Are you more concerned with what they'll think of you than you are about what Jesus thinks about your worship? Are you striving to be one of those that the "Father seeks to be His worshipers?"[25]

Or are you, as Paul later said, "now seeking the favor of men, or of God? Or am I striving to please men? If I were still trying to please men, I would not be a bond-servant of Christ."[26]

Who are you serving?

Who are you worshiping in your church?

Or, to cut to the chase, who in the account we just looked at represents you? Are you Mary? Or are you more like Peter and John?

Are you **Loving Jesus** or are you **Loving Church**?

This book is pretty much over. The choice is yours.

Now, choose wisely!

fineto

ENDNOTES—
AND OTHER STUFF THAT BELONGS AT THE END

How to continue your Love Jesus, Hate Church journey

endnotes

PREFACE: THE WELL-OILED MACHINE

1   Matthew 5:13-16
2   Revelation 2:5
3   Hebrews 11:38
4   Ephesians 3:20-21 (*italics and question mine*)
5   Matthew 16:18
6   John 10:10
7   *Scripture Alone*. Not traditions, best-selling books, or the teachings from popular preachers. It's God's Word and God's Word, alone.
8   Philippians 4:7
9   2 Timothy 3:5
10 Revelation 3:16
11 Mark 8:34 and many other related Scriptures that teach the same truth. In order to live for Christ we must die to self. There's no other way around it. Yes, the gift of salvation is free— in respect to the fact that we can't buy it, don't deserve it or can't earn it. But it is not free in regards to its cost.

Question: What does the gift of salvation cost me?
Answer: Me. Like, duh! All that I am in exchange for all that He is.
That's why the Bible states that we are not made better in Christ but are
buried with Him (death) and raised in His image to a new, *born again*
life. But we'll deal with this and other such subjects in much more
detail later on in the book. Just hang tight.

¹² Philippians 1:27

INTRODUCTION: THE JOY OF BELIEVING THE LIE

¹ Well, not exactly like Poe's story. It's a bit over the top. But I'll give
you some of the story anyway…

> *"TRUE! nervous, very, very dreadfully nervous I had been
> and am; but why WILL you say that I am mad? The disease
> had sharpened my senses, not destroyed, not dulled them.
> Above all was the sense of hearing acute. I heard all things
> in the heaven and in the earth. I heard many things in hell.
> How then am I mad? Hearken! and observe how healthily,
> how calmly, I can tell you the whole story."*
>
> *From the Tell-Tale Heart*

² What? Do you doubt my salvation because I would write a book that
unearths those who **Love Jesus** and **Hate Church**? Well, I understand.
It's natural. In fact, I probably would have felt the same way you do
a couple of years ago had I not come to the understanding that the hurt
in church must stop. And, if the only way to defuse the lie is with the
truth— then we need a book like **Love Jesus, Hate Church**.
By the way, if you want to know how I came to know Christ— my
testimony per se, just read the chapter titled **Tales From the Crypt**. I
think all your questions about my sincerity will be answered within
those pages. Later.

CHAPTER TWO: THE GOOD, THE BAD AND THE VERY UGLY

¹ Ephesians 1:4
² Revelation 3:16
³ John 10:10
⁴ 1 John 4:4
⁵ Matthew 19:26

6   John 17:20
7   Matthew 13:22
8   John 4:23
9   Acts 2:42-47

Chapter Three: Church Sucks!— and Other Prophetic Bumper Stickers

1   Revelation 3:16
2   Ephesians 3:20-21 (*italics and question mine*)
3   Matthew 16:18
4   John 10:10
5   Revelation 2:5
6   Matthew 16:18 (*italics mine*)
7   Acts 1:6
8   Matthew 16:13
9   Matthew 16:14
10   Matthew 16:15
11   Matthew 16:16
12   Matthew 16:18
13   Acts 2:42-47

Chapter Four: "I Can't Stop My Mouth!"

1   Luke 24:49
2   Acts 2:1
3   Acts 2:13
4   Acts 4:13 (*comments mine*)
5   Acts 2:36 (*italics mine*)
6   Acts 2:37
7   Acts 2:38
8   Ephesians 3:20-21 (*italics mine*)
9   Matthew 16:18
10   John 10:10 again…
11   Acts 4:20 – You know, I love these guys. Don't you?
12   Matthew 28:19
13   2 Corinthians 5:17
14   Luke 9:23

[15] Fay, Bill, "*Share Jesus Without Fear*", Nashville, TN, Broadman and Holman, June 1999.

[16] Ephesians 1:4-8

[17] Ephesians 1:5, 9

[18] Now, I know there is much more I could have written about the act of justification and the nature of Sam's faith placed in Christ. In fact, I may have even raised more questions than I have answered. But, as not to run a rabbit trail, I decided to put this entire paragraph in the "Cliff Notes" mode. My apologies to those who felt I should have explored this issue further— and I will. But that's for another time and another book.

[19] Matthew 28:19

[20] Matthew 28:19-20

[21] 1 Corinthians 6:20

CHAPTER FIVE: TALES FROM THE CRYPT

[1] Revelation 2:3-4

[2] I know it's not the same thing and I don't want to make any unfair comparisons, but I like to refer to my church battle scars as my "brand marks of Christ". You know, like Paul did in his letter to the Galatians.

[3] Romans 6:4 among others.

CHAPTER SIX: OB-LA-DI, OB-LA-DA, LIFE GOES ON...

[1] Matthew 7:11

[2] Daniel 5:25

[3] Emphasis mine.

[4] John 1:1

[5] John 3:3 (*emphasis and comments mine*)

[6] John 3:6

[7] Hebrews 4:12

CHAPTER SEVEN: I'LL NEVER EAT AT SHONEY'S AGAIN

[1] Oh, sound's a bit like Cedric the Entertainer. And looking back, I guess he was.

CHAPTER EIGHT: EMBITTERED RAGE OF THE SPIRIT

1 John 3:19
2 1 John 1:6

CHAPTER NINE: WE GOT LOTTO MO!

1 Ezekiel 1:4
2 Ezekiel 1:10
3 Ezekiel 1:22-28
4 Ezekiel 1:27-28
5 Acts 9:1-9
6 Ezekiel 2:1-2a
7 Ezekiel 2:2b-5 (*italics mine*)
8 Mathew 5:13-16
9 Ezckiel 2:4-5 (*paraphrase mine*)
10 Matthew 28:19-20
11 Acts 4:19-20
12 Matthew 28:19-20
13 Matthew 28:19-20
14 Ezekiel 2:4-7
15 Ezekiel 3:4-5
16 Ezekiel 3:6-7 (*italics mine*)
17 Ezckiel 3:8-11
18 Ezekiel 3:12-14
19 Ezekiel 3:14
20 Revelation 3:16
21 See the chapter titled, *Holy Crap— and Other Sermons by Frank Barone*, to develop our addiction to Bumper Sticker theology further.
22 Exodus 19:4
23 Revelation 2:4
24 Ezekiel 3:17
25 Ezekiel 3:18-19
26 Genesis 4:9
27 Ephesians 4:14-15
28 Revelation 3:15-19 (*italics and comments mine*)
29 Proverbs 24:12

CHAPTER TEN: RESCUE THOSE WHO ARE PERISHING

[1] Luke 9:62

[2] Revelation 3:16

[3] Warren, Rick, *"The Purpose Driven Life"*, Grand Rapids, Michigan, Zondervan, 2002.
Ok, hang on to your hat and let's look at the Purpose Driven way of salvation. Uh, can you see if anything is missing?
After spending two paragraphs condensing the Gospel into a simple Believe and Receive formula, the Purpose Driven Gospel Presentation moves to the closing prayer of repentance and faith.

From the pen of Rick Warren:
Wherever you are reading this, I invite you to bow your head and quietly whisper the prayer that will change your eternity: *"Jesus, I believe in you and I receive you."* Go ahead.
If you sincerely meant that prayer, congratulations! Welcome to the family of God! You are now ready to discover and start living God's purpose in your life.

From there, the reader is instructed to email Rick and receive a free booklet from his ministry. No repentance. No recognition of the Lordship of Christ. Nothing.
For me, it's Gospel Lite. "Same great taste, but less filling."

[4] 2 Timothy 4:3

[5] Proverbs 24:12

[6] Revelation 3:16

CHAPTER ELEVEN: TWO TRUTHS, TWO PATHS— ONE CHOICE

[1] Matthew 16:18

[2] Acts 10:34

[3] Exodus 34:28-35

[4] Ah, from *Jesus Christ, Superstar*. Remember?

[5] Revelation 1:6

[6] 1 Peter 2:9

[7] Remember him? He was the one with the strange, handlebar mustache.

[8] Acts 2:1-4

[9] 1 John 3:21-22

¹⁰ 2 Corinthians 5:20
¹¹ Hebrews 11 - Read the *whole* chapter. Twice.
¹² Ephesians 1:13-14
¹³ Matthew 5:14-16
¹⁴ John 14:16-17; - "I will ask the Father, and He will give you another Helper, that He may be with you forever; that is the Spirit of truth, whom the world cannot receive, because it does not see Him or know Him, but you know Him because He abides with you and will be in you."
¹⁵ Luke 24:48-49
¹⁶ Acts 2:1-4

Chapter Twelve: I'm a Fan of the Fanatics

¹ Romans 6:8
² 1 Corinthians 6:20
³ Luke 6:31
⁴ 1 Timothy 6:10
⁵ Acts 2:4-45 *(italics mine)*
⁶ From one of my favorite Brando movies, *On the Waterfront.*
⁷ You know, the stuff we do each Sunday— the service, choir, business meetings, revivals, VBS, mission trips, building projects, committee meetings… ad nauseam.
⁸ Ephesians 1:22-23 *(comments mine)*
⁹ Galatians 5:19-21
¹⁰ 1 Corinthians 1:11-12 - For I have been informed concerning you, my brethren, by Chloe's people, that there are quarrels among you. Now I mean this, that each one of you is saying, "I am of Paul," and "I of Apollos," and "I of Cephas," and "I of Christ."
¹¹ 1 Corinthians 3:1-7 - And I, brethren, could not speak to you as to spiritual men, but as to men of flesh, as to infants in Christ. I gave you milk to drink, not solid food; for you were not yet able to receive it. Indeed, even now you are not yet able, *for* you are still fleshly. For since there is jealousy and strife among you, are you not fleshly, and are you not walking like mere men? For when one says, "I am of Paul," and another, "I am of Apollos," are you not mere men? What then is Apollos? And what is Paul? Servants through whom you believed, even as the Lord gave opportunity to each one. I planted, Apollos watered,

but God was causing the growth. So then neither the one who plants nor the one who waters is anything, but God who causes the growth.

[12] 1 Corinthians 6:1-11 - Does any one of you, when he has a case against his neighbor, dare to go to law before the unrighteous and not before the saints? Or do you not know that the saints will judge the world? If the world is judged by you, are you not competent to constitute the smallest law courts? Do you not know that we will judge angels? How much more matters of this life? So if you have law courts dealing with matters of this life, do you appoint them as judges who are of no account in the church? I say this to your shame. Is it so, that there is not among you one wise man who will be able to decide between his brethren, but brother goes to law with brother, and that before unbelievers? Actually, then, it is already a defeat for you, that you have lawsuits with one another. Why not rather be wronged? Why not rather be defrauded? On the contrary, you yourselves wrong and defraud. You do this even to your brethren. Or do you not know that the unrighteous will not inherit the kingdom of God? Do not be deceived; neither fornicators, nor idolaters, nor adulterers, nor effeminate, nor homosexuals, nor thieves, nor the covetous, nor drunkards, nor revilers, nor swindlers, will inherit the kingdom of God. Such were some of you; but you were washed, but you were sanctified, but you were justified in the name of the Lord Jesus Christ and in the Spirit of our God.

[13] 1 Corinthians 6:7-8

[14] 2 Corinthians 12:20-21 - For I am afraid that perhaps when I come I may find you to be not what I wish and may be found by you to be not what you wish; that perhaps there will be strife, jealousy, angry tempers, disputes, slanders, gossip, arrogance, disturbances; I am afraid that when I come again my God may humiliate me before you, and I may mourn over many of those who have sinned in the past and not repented of the impurity, immorality and sensuality which they have practiced.

[15] Proverbs 20:19

[16] Philippians 4:2-3 - I urge Euodia and I urge Syntyche to live in harmony in the Lord. Indeed, true companion, I ask you also to help these women who have shared my struggle in the cause of the gospel, together with Clement also and the rest of my fellow workers, whose names are in the book of life.

Chapter Thirteen: Projectile Vomit— and the Sunday Morning Worship Service

[1] The Bible was written by design. Hence, nothing happens in it by chance. As a matter of fact, if a Sovereign God who lives beyond our time domain has the ability, which He does, to transcend time and see the end from the beginning as the Bible specifically says He does, then one way He would most likely communicate His existence to us from outside our time domain is to tell us beforehand what is going to happen in the future. Sound confusing? Well, really it's not. We call that prophecy.

All prophecy is of God, who sees the end from the beginning, revealing to us towards the beginning of an event what's going to happen at the end of the event. And when it happens, we sit back and say in amazement, "Wow, only God could know that!" That's why there are so many Old Testament prophecies about Jesus fulfilled in the New Testament. Hundreds of them. The simple fact of the hundreds of fulfilled prophecies about Jesus, and that fact alone, should be enough for most people to realize that He is the one and only Sovereign Lord— the Son of God.

We can also clearly see the imprint of God all throughout Scripture. Its intelligent design is undeniable. This marvelous design, by One outside our time domain, unmistakably points again to the fact that God is the Author of this Bible and it holds a mother-load of prophetic treasures for us today. In other words, Scripture speaks for the time when it was written and also for a future time, a prophetic time yet to be fulfilled. And that just blows the socks off me!

Let's take, for example, the book of the Revelation. The entire layout and focus of the book can be found, in summary form, in the very first chapter. "Write therefore the things which you have seen (Revelation 1, past-tense) and the things which are (chapters 2 and 3, current situation) and the things which shall take place after these things (Revelation 4 through the end of the book, future events). In the "things which are" section of the Revelation scheme, Jesus tells John to write seven letters to seven churches that were viable at that time and struggling with certain issues. To four of these churches, Ephesus, Pergamum, Thyatira, and Sardis, the Lord had both good and bad things to say about them. For two of these churches, Smyrna and Philadelphia, the Lord offered only His fondest praise for them. Yet, to one of the churches, the church at Laodicea, our Lord had absolutely nothing good, pleasant or edifying to say about them. Nothing. Their report card was an **F**. For them, the final church, the Lord Jesus reserved His harshest rebuke. And this is the church time in which we live. I called it the **Love Jesus**, **Hate Church** age of the church.

2   Revelation 3:14-17 (*question mine*)
3   Revelation 3:16
4   Revelation 3:17
5   Revelation 3:17b
6   John 15:8
7   John 2:24
8   Revelation 3:16
9   Joshua 24:15 (*emphasis and comments mine*)
10   1 John 4:4
11   John 10:10

CHAPTER FOURTEEN: WHAT WE CALL NORMAL, AIN'T NORMAL

1   Matthew 23:11
2   John 13:3-5
3   John 14:1-3
4   Matthew 5:42
5   Matthew 6:25-34
6   Matthew 5:39
7   Matthew 18:21-22
8   Matthew 13:44 (*italics mine*)
9   Matthew 13:45-46 (*italics mine*)
10   James 4:4
11   Romans 8:5-9
12   John 15:18-19
13   Romans 7:18-25
14   Ephesians 2:4-7
15   Revelation 2:1
16   Revelation 3:16
17   John 10:10

CHAPTER FIFTEEN: HOLY CRAP! AND OTHER SERMONS BY FRANK BARONE

1 John 10:10
2 Matthew 8:20
3 1 Timothy 1:15
4 Ephesians 1:13-14
5 Revelation 3:16
6 Matthew 5:48
7 1 Timothy 4:1
8 Revelation 3:16
9 1 Timothy 1:11
10 Matthew 5:48
11 1 Peter 1:14-16 *(italics mine)*
12 Romans 1:7
13 1 Corinthians 1:2
14 2 Corinthians 1:1
15 Ephesians 1:18
16 Philippians 4:22
17 Colossians 1:2
18 Ephesians 2:13-14
19 Leviticus 11:45 *(question and italics mine)*
20 Leviticus 19:1-2 *(question and italics mine)*
21 Leviticus 20:7-8 *(questions and italics mine)*
22 Ezekiel 36:22-23 *(italics mine)*
23 Malachi 1:11 *(once again, italics mine)*
24 1 John 1:6
25 Luke 6:46
26 John 14:15-17 *(question and italics mine)*
27 John 14:21 *(questions and italics mine)*

CHAPTER SIXTEEN: "HEY, I COULDA BEEN A CONTENDER!"

1 Revelation 2:5
2 Matthew 13:3-9
3 Matthew 5:48 *(italics mine)*
4 John 10:10
5 1 John 1:5
6 1 John 1:6 *(comments and italics mine)*

7   Vintage, *Let's Make a Deal*— which was one of the most popular television game shows during the 1960's and 70's. Monty's Cookie Jar was one of the grand prize options. And Monty refers to Monty Hall, the show's host and co-creator.

8   2 Timothy 3:1-5

9   Matthew 7:21-23 (*question and italics mine*)

10 1 Corinthians 7:1 (*italics mine*)

11 1 Peter 1:14-16 (*italics mine*)

12 Exodus 20:1-11

13 1 John 1:6

14 Isaiah 64:6

15 John 4:23-24

CHAPTER SEVENTEEN: BURGER KING, FRENCH FRIES AND THE KINGDOM OF GOD

1   John 10:10 – once again. Ahem.

2   Acts 4:13

3   Ephesians 3:20-21 (*italics mine*)

4   1 Corinthians 6:20

5   Ephesians 1:14

6   Romans 8:2

7   These are from Neil Anderson's, *Steps to Freedom in Christ*, Regal Books, 3rd Edition, October 2004. It is a *must* read for anyone who doesn't want to be crushed by the prevailing **Love Jesus, Hate Church** sentiment.

8   Matthew 18:3

CHAPTER EIGHTEEN: PEOPLE DO WHAT THEY WANT TO DO

1   John 10:10

2   John 4:23

3   Against my better judgment I have changed the name of the church to protect the, well… the *guilty*. But the time, town, conversations and other dark details are true. Shame on you.

4   Proverbs 12:15 and 21:1 among others.

5   Galatians 5:16

6   Numbers 20:10

7   1 Samuel 13:14

[8] 2 Samuel 12:7
[9] Luke 2:15
[10] Revelation 3:16

CHAPTER NINETEEN: LATEX GLOVES AND HANDS-ON MINISTRY

[1] Matthew 8:2-4
[2] Matthew 8:14-15
[3] Mark 5:35-43
[4] Matthew 9:27-31
[5] Mark 7:31-35
[6] Matthew 19:13-15

CHAPTER TWENTY: IS MASTURBATION A SIN?

[1] Matthew 15:7-9
[2] Joshua 24:15

CHAPTER TWENTY-ONE: WHO YOU GONNA CALL? CHURCHBUSTERS!

[1] Psalm 115:3. My favorite verse, by the way.
[2] What's even more disheartening for the pastor or other church leaders is
the fact that because of the constitutional structure of most churches—
the Constitution and By-Laws that were literally written by these
very people themselves— in most cases the "small print" in these sacred
documents simply won't allow you the freedom to remove them from
their strategic *gatekeeping* position.
There's just no easy way to vote them out... or off.

Now, if it takes two-thirds (or even a simple majority for that matter)
of the membership of a church to change the Constitution or By-Laws,
and if you only average about 125 on a Sunday, and if two-thirds of the
membership is over 600 people... well, you do the math. It's virtually
impossible, save a burning-bush intervention from above, to change the
Constitution. Therefore it stands.
Which translated means: Deacons who "deac" without term limits. Lifelong, self-perpetuating Elders that only resign when they are carried out

feet first. Business Meetings that become the focus of Sunday and not the worship of the Lord.

"Hey, it's the way we did business in 1948 and, by God, we ain't 'bout to change it now!"

How do you go about trying to change this impasse?

How does one try to move the church from the altar of self-gratification to the foot of Christ's cross?

How?

Honestly, you can't. It takes some outside help.

Churchbusters!

Chapter Twenty-Two: Blowing Snot Bubbles

1   John 4:23 (*italics mine*)
2   Luke 7:39
3   Luke 7:44-50
4   John 14:27
5   Philippians 4:7
6   1 Corinthians 6:19-20
7   Matthew 26:35, 74
8   John 1:9; 1 John 2:8
9   John 20:11
10   John 20:2
11   John 20:2b
12   John 20:3
13   John 12:25
14   Matthew 26:33
15   John 20:10
16   Galatians 6:7
17   Matthew 10:33
18   John 20:11
19   John 20:13
20   John 20:14
21   John 20:15
22   John 20:17
23   Luke 7:50
24   Matthew 5:14-16
25   John 4:23
26   Galatians 1:10

one final thought...

I call heaven and earth to witness against you today,
that I have set before you life and death,
the blessing and the curse.

So choose life in order that you may live,
you and your descendants.
Deuteronomy 30:19

Oh yeah, choose life!
Choose wiscly!
Just choose.

For more information about **Love Jesus**, **Hate Church** or for
additional resources, please contact us at:

info@lovejesushatechurch.com
www.lovejesushatechurch.com

BACK2ACTS

P R O D U C T I O N S

presents

LOVE JESUS HATE CHURCH

HOW TO **SURVIVE** IN CHURCH— OR **DIE** TRYING!

CHURCH SEMINAR

WITH

STEVE MCCRANIE

For booking information and details, contact:

INFO@LOVEJESUSHATECHURCH.COM
WWW.LOVEJESUSHATECHURCH.COM